A CALL TO LOVE

Crimson Cross Publishing L.L.C.

New Orleans, LA.

Unless otherwise indicated, any reference to Scripture in this book has been taken from the Holy Bible: King James Version.

Unless otherwise indicated, Biblical words are defined by Strong's Exhaustive Concordance of the Bible.

ISBN: 978-1-7349230-0-1

PRINTED IN THE UNITED STATES OF AMERICA.

DEDICATION

As a very young child, prior to the age of seven,
before I really knew or understood anything about Jesus, or God, or Christianity, there were
three women that really stood out in my life. There was always something about these ladies that
was strong, and quiet, and peaceful, and different. It wasn't until years later that I understood
why they stood out. It was because of their Christianity and their dedication to it. Their names
are Ethel (Mrs. Ethel) Brown, Minnie (Mrs. Bell) Johnson and Henrietta (Aunt Baby)
Anderson. Although all of these women are deceased now, they were, in essence, my introduction
to the living God.

From the age of eight until I was well into my teens,
there was another woman that stood out in my life. I didn't know it then, but watching her
proclaim her love for Christ through her good times and through her intensely bad times had a
profound effect on me and was actually a major factor in guiding me toward the living God. She
was my mom's closest friend and her name is Johnnie M. August. Her solid belief in God
helped to solidify
my belief in Him.

In my late twenties, after having been a baptized believer
for almost ten years, at the point when I had finally decided to begin the journey of living my
life for Christ, there was yet another woman that came along and stood out. Back then I had no
idea what to do as a Christian or even how to be a Christian, but this woman took me under
her wing and taught me as much as I would allow her. Her name is Audrey M. Palmer and
her steadfast living for Christ was the anchor that rooted me in Him.

These five women allowed God to use them in one way or another
to let me know that He had been there with me from the very beginning, leading me, guiding
me, lighting my path to Him. Because of their obedience and dedication to our Father, even in
their times of struggle, this book is dedicated to each of them.

"You were the lights that helped to lead me out of darkness and for that reason,
from the bottom of my heart, I say thank you!"

^{1st} Corinthians 13:4-8(KJV)

Love suffereth long, and is kind; Love envieth not; Love vaunteth not itself, is not puffed up,
Doth not behave itself unseemly, seeketh not her own, is not easily provoked, thinketh no evil;
Rejoiceth not in iniquity, but rejoiceth in the truth;
Beareth all things, believeth all things, hopeth all things, endureth all things.
Love never faileth:

FOREWORD

"…but I have called you friends; for all things that I have heard of my Father I have made known unto you."
(John 15:15 KJV)

Has anyone ever really sat down and explained what Christianity is?

For me, that answer would be a resounding no. I was told that I should be a Christian. That was explained to me in detail. I was told all the things I could not do as a Christian. That list of don'ts was overwhelming. I was even told how to become a Christian. Repeatedly.

The one thing I was not ever told, however, is what Christianity is.

Over the years, years of studying the bible, trials and tribulation, going to church, fasting, crying out to God, praying, praising God, and walking with Christ, I have come to see exactly what Christianity is. Not just the part about being saved, because it's so much more than that. Not just the part about receiving blessings, it's so much deeper than that. No, I have come to see Christianity in its depth and in its simplicity. I have come to see it in its greatness and in its splendor. I have come to know it in its beauty and in all of its perfection. And every time I see it, every time I think about it, I am in absolute awe of God.

As I began to understand Christianity, I came to the realization that not many Christians can live it or walk it out successfully without first *knowing* what it is and then having a clear *understanding* of what it is. No matter how hard we may try, no matter how much we may desire in our hearts to live out this life, without knowing what we have become involved in we are bound to fail.

So I'm going to take what it took me years to learn, what God spent years teaching me, and I'm going to put it all right here. I'm going to freely share with you what God so freely shares with us all.

Christianity.

What Christianity is.

So, let's begin at the beginning…

Chapter One

What Is Christianity?

Let this mind be in you, which was also in Christ Jesus:
Who, being in the form of God, thought it not robbery to be equal with God:
But made himself of no reputation, and took upon him the form of a servant, and was
made in the likeness of men:
And being found in fashion as a man, he humbled himself, and became obedient
unto death, even the death of the cross.
(Philippians 2:5-8 KJV)

Christianity.
What exactly is it?
Simply put, Christianity is a call to love.

It is God calling you, assigning you, and trusting you, to be a demonstration and a reflection of His love while you're here on this earth. Christianity is an agreement between you and God in which you willingly agree to accept His Son as your savior. Christianity is a promise between you and God in which you willingly agree to use the life He has blessed you with as a ministry to bring as many to Christ as you can. And Christianity is a covenant between you and God in which you willingly agree to be a living manifestation of Christ just as Christ was and is a living manifestation of God.

Christianity is a call to love.

Christianity Is A Call To Love What?

It is a call to love God. It is a call to love God's people.

Yep, that's it. It's just that simple.

However, the simplicity of its description does not mean there is simplicity in acting it out. Why? Because you can't act out what you don't know and what a lot of us don't know is what love is. In fact, what most of us do not know is that Christianity and humanity have two different definitions of love, definitions that produce fruit, definitions that produce results.

One type of love produces worldly fruit and worldly results while the other type of love produces spiritual fruit and spiritual results. One type of love oftentimes harms the church while the other type always edifies the church and glorifies God. However, without knowing that there is a difference in the types of love and without knowing what those differences are, demonstrating what is unknown and acting out what has not been taught or learned is almost impossible.

The Different Types of Love.

<u>Worldly Love.</u>

We, as humans, have created a definition of love that is mostly based on feelings. If we feel good about a person, we do good things with and for that person. The love we show a person is based on the emotion we have for them at any given moment. When our feelings change, the love changes. This difference in behavior happens because love, to us, is emotion based and it is, in all honesty, profit based.

If the love will, in some way, benefit us, we'll give it and we'll gladly receive it. However, if we will get nothing from that love, if it can't benefit us, we'll keep it to ourselves or reject it. With this type of love, we are looking for results that are beneficial to us and us alone.

<u>Christian Love.</u>

In Christianity, love is spirit based and action based. Therefore, the negative things you may feel about a person should not be a determining factor in whether or not you act out your love for that person. Your negative feelings should not be a determining factor in whether or not you act out your obedience to God concerning that person. In fact, your negativity toward an individual should have no bearing on whether or not you demonstrate love to and for that person at all. Whether you like them or not, as a Christian you are called to love them, to demonstrate Christ to them.

Why?

Because love, to God, is not *just* feeling based.

It is action based.

It is obedience based.

It is spirit based.

With this in mind, we should understand that Christian love is not for our benefit only, but for the benefit of the church and for the benefit of the people God created. When God calls upon us to complete the mission of love, there should be nothing that gets in our way concerning that. Self and self-benefit has to take a back seat and we must reflect God when it comes to His children.

The Calls of Love.

First and foremost, as a Christian, you are called to love God. You are called to love God with everything in you. In fact, scripture says:

> *"And thou shalt love the Lord thy God with all thy heart, and with all thy soul, and with all thy mind, and with all thy strength: this is the first commandment.*
> *(Mark 12:30 KJV)*

At this point we now know that love requires action and that means we should not only feel love for God, but we should also act it out. For many, here is where confusion comes in, here is where we begin to question how to act out love, especially love to God. We begin to wonder how we go about performing love when we've been so accustomed to just feeling it. But there is no need to wonder about that because God makes it clear in His word what we must do to demonstrate love to Him.

> *"If ye love me, keep my commandments."*
> *(John 14:15 KJV)*

Simple, isn't it?

Not exactly.

You see, keeping God's commandments requires us to know what God's commandments are. For us to know His commandments we are required to seek His commandments out. Seeking them out means we have to know where and how to seek them out. And even though one part of the seeking process is easy, the other part is not.

So, how do we find out what God's commandments are?

Well, the Bible is the first place to start. The Bible is the foundation, the beginning of spiritual knowledge, the most important place to see and learn the word of God. But the Bible isn't the *only* place to seek God's commandments. Aside from God's word, His commandments can also be sought out in prayer, in daily conversations with Him. In this intimate setting, you can and oftentimes will find commandments that are specific to your life, specific to your situation, specific to whatever God has gifted you with or to whatever God has called you to do.

However, along with prayer and daily conversations with God, you also have to know God's voice to know the commandments from Him when you hear them.

"My sheep hear my voice, and I know them, and they follow me:"
(John 10:27 KJV)

You have to know God well enough to differentiate between other voices, your own voice, and the voice of God. And that process does not come easy to many. In fact, it is a lifelong process that requires a desire to hear God, dedication, patience, and a listening ear. It also requires a deep and personal relationship with God, and that, too, is a lifelong process.

However, learning all of God's commandments in every way imaginable will not matter if a desire to obey is lacked. Why? Because you can know everything The Almighty says, know every commandment written in God's word, but if you don't have a heart for God, a desire for God, if you choose not to do any of what you have been commanded to do by God, it is all simply knowledge wasted and love denied. Because at the core of it all is love and love is unknown to everyone when it is only felt by you. It doesn't become known to anyone until you perform it.

<u>You Are Called To Love God's People.</u>

This one can be quite difficult.

Loving God's people is not the easiest thing in the world to do.

Sometimes it's because of the way we feel and sometimes it's because of the way people behave. Sometimes it's our pride, our ego, or our anger that stops us from loving someone the way we should. No matter the reason, however, we are commanded to love others. Therefore, nothing should stop us.

> *"And the second is like, namely this, Thou shalt love thy neighbour as thyself. There is none other commandment greater than these."*
> *(Mark 12:31 KJV)*

With this commandment in mind, we should understand that the level of difficulty sometimes required to love people should not be the reason or excuse we use to not love others. It should not be the reason that we don't fulfill God's commandment to love people.

We should also know that God is a God of purpose and loving others is for a purpose, for a Godly purpose. Sometimes we will understand that purpose and sometimes not. However, loving God's people is an absolute must in and for the church.

Love is an action verb and therefore requires action. Loving others requires us to not only feel love for them, but to *treat* them as if we love them. It requires us to allow God to love them through us. It requires us to do those things which will help them grow in Christ and elevate spiritually. Often, it may require us to sacrifice what we feel or need in favor of ensuring that they stay on the Godly path, or in favor of them *getting* on the Godly path. However, we must also know that in the midst of the sacrifice, we are learning and growing spiritually as well.

In essence, loving God's people is an assignment to love them out of captivity. You see, those who are unsaved, those who do not know the Lord, are captive. They are being held captive by the world, the things in and of this world, by the evil one, by people, by those they love, and sometimes even by themselves. To love them as a Christian should is to love the chains of captivity off of them, it is to love them until they know the truth because scripture says, *"And ye shall know the truth and the truth shall make you free.* (John 8:32 KJV)

On the flip side of that love token, loving others requires us to *never* be a hindrance to a Christian or to their relationship with God. It requires us to *never* put a stumbling block in the way of those already saved and of those that are trying to be saved. Loving others means *never* doing anything that will draw a person, their attention, or their focus away from Christ. Instead, it requires us to do those things that will always lead a person to Christ, to the church, and ultimately to God.

Bear in mind that there will be times when the act of love does not always feel good to you or to them, and times when the person on the receiving end may reject the love you are trying to give them. This happens because, as a Christian, you may be trying to show them Christian love and they may be accustomed to worldly love.

Christian love goes deeper than the feelings, deeper than the flesh. When a person is in a worldly mind state, a fleshly mind state, what you are doing or offering them in the spirit may offend them in the flesh, or it may even offend their actual flesh. This is why it is so important that feelings, negative feelings, never play a part in whether or not we show love to our neighbors. It should never affect whether or not we offer them the love of Christ through us. Because at the end of it all, it's not about us and how we feel, it's about God, loving God's people, and caring about the condition of their souls.

Therefore, to break it all down to its most simple form, Christianity is a call for each of us to love God and to love others. It is a call for us to demonstrate Christ, to be a reflection of Him to those who, otherwise, may never see Him. It is a call for us to introduce people to Christ so that through Christ they can come to know God.

It is a call to love.

Thus, a new question begs to be asked.

And that question is…

What is love?

CHAPTER TWO

What Is Love?

Though I speak with the tongues of men and of angels, and have not love, I am become as sounding brass, or a tinkling cymbal.
And though I have the gift of prophecy, and understand all mysteries, and all knowledge; and though I have all faith, so that I could remove mountains, and have not love, I am nothing.
1ˢᵗ Corinthians 13:1-2 (KJV)

A great deal of the previous chapter was spent telling you that you *should* love and touching a little upon how to do it. This chapter will tell you what love is, what we should love, how we should love, and why we should love.

So, let's begin this by asking a question.

What Is Love?

Love is the building of, and the edification of, the church and the Kingdom of God by the saving of souls.

And just how do we save souls?

We lead the person to Jesus. We love them. We rescue them from a world of hate by loving them. We love them out of captivity and into the kingdom, into the church, into the body of Christ. That love, that selfless, altruistic, agapé love will draw them nigh to Jesus Christ who is love incarnate. And Jesus Christ will save their souls.

Think about this for a second:

There once was a man who loved you so much that he heard about your suffering and decided to help you. Now in order to help you, this man had to leave the comforts and safety of his home to get to where you were, and where you were wasn't the nicest or safest of places.

This man lived in a mansion in the best part of town where there was no killing, no drama, no fighting. No stress and no worries. He lived in a home that had not only everything, but the *best of everything*. He was comfortable and safe at home. So, leaving his home, the comforts of his home, and the safety of his environment was a great deal for him.

However, he exchanged his comforts and his safety for your pain and your suffering. He left those comforts and went on a mission from a peaceful environment to a hostile environment. And he did it all so that he could save you, so that he could save you by bringing you home with him to the safe place, to the peaceful place.

He had everything and he wanted you to have everything too.

Once he got to where you were, he repeatedly placed himself in harm's way to pull you out of harm's way. Never considering himself in all of this, he talked to people for you, sacrificed for you. He was beaten for you, jailed for you. And eventually he was killed for you.

He exchanged his life for your own.

And his death saved your life.

Now, what do you call such an act? I would call it an act of love. And what would you call the person who would give so much of himself just to help you? I would call him Jesus.

Jesus, the Son of God.

Jesus, the true definition of love.

What Should You Love?

To answer this question all we have to do is look at the life of Jesus. In His life we can clearly see that what Jesus loved was God and God's people. And being Christians, that is what we should love as well.

God.

And God's people.

You see, when we study the life of Jesus, we see that in all Jesus did, He was showing us His love and God's love. He was demonstrating the definition of love in all of its perfection. He was offering us His undying, infinite, unconditional love. And to be a Christian means to be like Christ, to show God and others undying, infinite, unconditional love.

That should be very simple, right?

Not quite.

As Christians we struggle with this and we struggle with it hard.

Why the struggle?

I believe the struggle comes from the fact that Christian love comes with a cost and that cost is the ego, pride, and self. You see, to exemplify Christian love, more often than not you have to sacrifice your ego, your pride, and yourself, and most people struggle with sacrificing themselves for anything and for anyone. In fact, more often than not pride, ego, and self gets in the way when it comes to sacrificing self for any reason. But to love God's people as Christ loved and still loves means that you cannot have an ego, you cannot have pride, and you cannot have an exaggerated sense of self.

Loving God's people the way Christ did and for the reasons Christ did means that you cannot think more highly of self than you ought to. You can't think more highly of self than you think of others. And you definitely cannot think more highly of self than you think of God.

To break this down even farther, let's explain ego, pride, and an exaggerated sense of self by imagining that, concerning our salvation, God and Jesus had a conversation that went something like this:

God said, *"Son, I need you to go to earth and save my people. This will require you to hide your divinity in a new human shell. You will have to teach them things that they will be too stubborn to learn. You will have to show them things they will be too blind to see. You will have to tell them things they will be too deaf to hear.*

"Son, you will have to bear their sins and suffer for their sakes and still, a lot of them will not respect you or even appreciate you until it is much too late. However, for them to be saved, for them to spend eternity with Me, for them to not suffer the fires of Hell, this has to be done. You have to do this."

"But Father," says Jesus as He turns up His nose at His Father's words, *"You are God and I am Your Son, the Son of the Most High. I am royalty. I am divine. It is far beneath me to shed my perfection and take upon myself their imperfections. It is beneath me to go there, to that treacherous place, to save people that You have just said are stubborn, blind, and deaf.*

"If they choose not to be with You, that is their problem. I don't have that problem, so why should I debase myself for them, for people that are far beneath Me? And why should I, Your only begotten Son, make their problems my problems? I am Jesus, those people are nothing compared to me. Besides, You have Me. Why do You want them?"

If Jesus had an ego, if Jesus had pride, if Jesus had an exaggerated sense of self, that is what their conversation would have been like. Because Jesus would have loved Himself more than He loved God and more than He loved God's people, *if* He loved God and *if* He loved God's people *at all*.

And if Jesus *did have* that ego, *did have* that pride, *did have* that exaggerated sense of self, where would we be right now? What would be the condition of our souls? What would be the final destination of our souls? Ultimately, when everything was all said and done, where would be fated to spend eternity? The same place the lost and unsaved would be headed if we let ego, pride, and an exaggerated sense of self stop us from loving God's people the way we have been called to.

If ye love me, keep my commandments.
(John 14:15 KJV)

Jesus clearly stated that if you love Him you would keep His commandments. Thus, we can clearly see that if this story was real, had Jesus not obeyed God, He would have demonstrated a clear lack of love not only for God, but also for God's people.

It is for that reason that the ego can have no part in exhibiting Christian love. Ego kills love. Ego steals love. Ego destroys love. Thinking too highly of ourselves stops us from thinking highly of others. Having ourselves as the main focus prevents us from having anyone else as the main focus. And if Christ had no ego when it came to us, shouldn't we have no ego when it comes to God, when it comes to Christ, and when it comes to others?

How Should You Love?

We should love by using our lives as our ministry.

You see, knowing that Christianity is a call for us to love, to save souls by edifying and building the church, we have to use the life God gave us to exhibit that love, to build that church. We have to purpose to do, say, and be what is right according to God and His word, not according to our feelings or our flesh.

Doing what is right in the presence of everyone is love. It shows that you love them enough to never introduce that which is wrong to them. It shows that you love them enough to demonstrate love when the world around you is a perfect demonstration of hate. And it shows that, through you and others like you, God is still alive and well and walking this earth.

It also teaches those who may not already know, the difference between right and wrong. Living righteously among others demonstrates what righteousness is in a world where unrighteousness seems to reign supreme. Humbling ourselves and being obedient to God in the presence of so much pride and disobedience demonstrates love to all who may be watching.

How?

Because being obedient to God will never lead a person to damnation. Our obedience exhibits love, and love can and will only lead people to salvation. That's why we must obey the word of God at all times. That's why our lives are our ministry, a ministry we should use to love others and to lead others to Christ.

What we do with our lives, people see.

What people see, they do.

What people do will determine their salvation or their damnation.

So, how should we love?

We should love by using our lives as our ministry. Our ministry is love. And love is what saves souls.

Why Should You Love?

First and foremost, you should love God.

And you should love God because He first loved us and because He commanded us to.

> *And thou shalt love the Lord thy God with all thine heart, and with all thy soul,*
> *and with all thy might.*
> *(Deuteronomy 6:5 KJV)*

We should love God because He loved us enough to create us. He loved us enough to breathe His very breath into us and bless us with the gift of life. When we were doomed to damnation, He loved us enough to save us. He loved us enough to send His very own Son to this world to suffer for us so we didn't have to. And He loved us enough that through the suffering of His very own son, our souls would be saved and reconciled to him for all eternity.

And that is just the beginning of the reasons we should love God.

If we remember all of the things God has done for us since the day we were born, there would be no less than a million more reasons to love Him with every breath we take.

When it comes to loving God's people, though, we should love them because there is a world of them that are dying. Their hearts are dying because they are filled with lust, lusting after things and after people instead of being filled with love for God. Their minds are dying because they are focused on those things that can only bring temporary happiness instead of being focused on Godly things, Godly things that will not only sustain them and keep them alive while they are here, but things that will keep them alive and with God for eternity.

Their flesh is dying as they are doing those things that help them to fit into this world, a world in which they really do not belong. They are dying to be loved, dying to be accepted, dying to be wanted by a people who can only take them as far as death leads them. They are dying and God has commanded us to love them so that they may live.

And we should love them because at the end of the day, if we are not loving God's people, we are being active participants in the death of those people.

This is my commandment, That ye love one another, as I have loved you.
(John 15:12 KJV)

In Summation...

To love people, as the Bible says, is not to make sure everyone has warm fuzzy feelings. To show Christian love is to make sure the condition of their soul is good with God, and to do things that would draw them nearer to God. Showing Christian love is not to make them feel more comfortable in the world or in doing worldly things, it is to secure their place in eternity with God.

Jesus came here and did not go out of His way to make people feel all warm and fuzzy. He did what He could to save our souls to the point that He made people so *un*comfortable they killed Him for that discomfort.

However, Christ functioned in love.

He loved God enough to do God's will to the point of His own death. And He loved *us* enough to do Gods will to the point of His own death. Christ walked in love and thus, when we become Christians, we are called to do the same.

To love.

Because Christianity calls us to.

CHAPTER THREE

What Is the Purpose of Christianity?

"Where there is no vision, the people perish:"
Proverbs 29:18 (KJV)

What is the purpose of Christianity?

The purpose of Christianity is to fulfil God's vision for humanity.

Yep, it's that simple. God created us with a vision in mind, a holy vision He desires to see out to the very end.

And what exactly is that vision?

Again, it is much simpler than people make it out to be. God's vision is that we should all enjoy eternity with Him and that none of us should perish, not one. He longs to spend eternity with each and every one of us.

How do we know this is God's vision?

Because He told us in His holy word.

The Lord is not slack concerning his promise, as some men count slackness; but is longsuffering to us-ward, not willing that any should perish, but that all should come to repentance.
(2nd Peter 3:9 KJV)

There it is.
Crystal clear.
The purpose of Christianity.

For most of us, however, Christianity was only thought of as something we should attain. That's it. And once we were saved, we were to live out our lives waiting on God to bless us and learning to depend on Him for everything.

However, that's not exactly what Christianity is all about.

In truth, Christianity is about much more than becoming saved. It's about doing all you can do to bring others to salvation as well. We don't just get saved to be saved, we get saved so that we can use our saved lives as a ministry to lead others to Christ.

Becoming saved is just the beginning of Christianity.

It is not the entirety of Christianity.

Fulfilling God's vision is the entirety of Christianity.

A perfect example of that vision is clearly displayed in the creation. Before Adam and Eve, God took the time to create everything else first. The Heavens, the earth, the animals, the sun, the moon, the garden. Everything. Then He created Adam and placed him in a world where everything was already available to him and at his fingertips. Even God Himself.

There was no struggle, no strife, no stress. No distractions that would keep Adam focused on anything other than God. Only a garden that Adam was commanded to keep, to maintain, and a close relationship with God. Adam was so close to God that God brought every beast of the field and every fowl of the air to him to see what Adam would name them. They talked. They communed. God knew Adam. Adam knew God. That's how close God and Adam were. That's how close God wants to be to and with us.

Why?

Because He loves us.

In addition to that closeness, God wanted Adam to have someone just for him. Thus, Eve was created as well. So, not only did Adam have everything he could ever need in that garden, now he had the perfect someone, someone created especially for him, to share that garden with.

He had every*thing*.

He had Eve.

And he had God.

Adam had his own private Heaven, his own private eternity with the Father because that's the way God envisioned it to be. That was how He planned it, that was how it was supposed to be with Adam, that is how it is supposed to be with us.

Enter Jesus.

You see, Adam was the reason for the separation from God, but God never intended for us to be separated from Him. That's why the need for Jesus exists. Jesus is the reason for our reconnection with God.

Throughout the Old Testament, after Adam and Eve were removed from the garden, the disconnect from God became so rampant, the people were so wicked and so violent, that God destroyed them with a great flood. All that were left was Noah and his family.

The destruction that came upon the people back then represented the destruction that would come upon those of us who, today, reject God, reject Christ. The fact that only Noah's family was left when it was all said and done represents the fact that only God's family will be left when everything with this current world is all said and done.

There were eight people left post flood. Eight is the number of new beginnings. Noah's family was the new beginning back then. God's family, every person that is saved, will be the new beginning when this earth passes away. And His vision is that we would *all* be a part of His family.

Just based on what God did with Noah and his household, it is clear that God loved us so much back then that even when He destroyed the *wickedness* of His people, He didn't destroy the *good* of the people. Through Noah and that goodness, He gave us another chance, another chance at reconciliation with Him. Today, it is only through Jesus that we get another chance at reconciliation with Him. That is how much He desires to be with us, desires us to be with Him.

That was His vision then and it is still His vision now.

Because He loves us.

And that is why He wants us to draw others to Christ.

Because He loves them too.

After the flood came the enslavement of God's people by the Egyptians. That enslavement back then represents the enslavement the world has over God's people today. Enslavement of the minds and of the hearts and of the actions. God sent a savior to free them from the Egyptians back then. Moses. Today, our Savior is Jesus. He was sent to save us from the world and its enslavement of our minds, of our hearts, and of our actions.

Not only did Moses bring about freedom from enslavement, but through him came the laws. Not just the ten commandments, but a total of six hundred-thirteen commandments that God wanted us to adhere to. The creation of the laws, however, was done so that we could clearly see that we were unable to fulfill those laws without God. It was to magnify our flaws and faults, letting us know that only God was righteous and that with Him we too would be righteous. It was to show us that we needed God, to bring us closer to Him. Just the way He envisions it to be.

The laws were also to show us that the knowledge of good and evil that we had attained from Adam's eating of the fruit was more than we were capable of handling. And that instead of leaning on what the fruit had produced in us, we should have been leaning on and trusting in God.

After the laws came the judges to assist in the enforcement of those laws and to keep God's people from being held captive, but even the judges had issues and at times failed God and His people.

All throughout the Old Testament, God repeatedly sent people to free us, to deliver us from captivity, at times to prevent us from being taken captive. We had priests, ceremonies, atonements, prophets, judges, and kings to bring us always back into good standing with God. Because God's desire for our connection with Him is magnificent in its strength.

However, no matter what He gave them, His people, they were oftentimes unable to be obedient, they were unable to and unwilling to get right with God. Sometimes they were unwilling to accept the reconnection and reconciliation to and with God, so to save them from them, to reconnect them to Him, He gave them Jesus.

The birth of Jesus.
The life of Jesus.
The crucifixion of Jesus.
The resurrection of Jesus.
The salvation of their souls.

> *My little children, these things write I unto you, that ye sin not.*
> *And if any man sin, we have an advocate with the Father, Jesus Christ the righteous:*
> *And he is the propitiation for our sins:*
> *and not for ours only, but also for the sins of the whole world.*
> *(1 John 2:1-2 KJV)*

In Jesus' life, He committed no sin, unlike the past prophets, judges and kings. He walked righteously, again unlike the past prophets, judges, and kings. He lived His life in absolute obedience to God, great obedience, even to the point of death.

He was continuously at one with God just as God wants us to be. As a result, Jesus, in His perfection, eliminated the need for repeated atonement whether it be daily, weekly, monthly or yearly. And for that reason, once we accept Jesus, we are eternally atoned, eternally at one with God. We are one with Jesus who is one with God.

To add to that perfection, because Jesus fulfilled the law, we no longer have to work to fulfill the law. Our belief in Jesus is the fulfilling of the law for us. However, that belief in Jesus does not give us free reign to sin, in fact just the opposite is true. Our belief in Jesus gives us free reign to love knowing that the love of Christ is cleansing, and any sinful desire should and will be shameful to us. Jesus' love, the depth of it, makes it almost impossible to *truly* desire God and to desire sin at the same time.

In addition, Jesus is not only the fulfilling of the law, He is also the fulfilling of God's vision. Through Him, we are saved and by Him we are called to assist others in becoming saved. That is why He gave us the great commission commandment.

And Jesus came and spake unto them, saying, All power is given unto me in heaven
and in earth.
Go ye therefore, and teach all nations, baptizing them in the name of the Father,
and of the Son, and of the Holy Ghost:
Teaching them to observe all things whatsoever I have commanded you: and, lo, I am
with you always, even unto the end of the world. Amen.
Matthew 28:18-20 (KJV)

In Summation...

Jesus is the reason for our salvation. The great commission calls for us to bring others to Jesus so that they too might be saved just as He wants them to be, just as God wants them to be. He gave us a calling and to execute that calling God gave us life. The very life that we live is our ministry. The ministry God gave us. The ministry that we have been called to use to fulfil God's vision.

The vision of Christianity.

The saving of souls.

CHAPTER FOUR

What Is A Christian?

For even hereunto were ye called: because Christ also suffered for us, leaving us an example, that ye should follow his steps:
1 Peter 2:21 (KJV)

What is a Christian?

Simply put, a Christian is one who follows and lives the teachings of Jesus Christ for the purpose of saving souls.

Why?

Because a Christian understands that our lives are not our own. A Christian understands that our lives have been exchanged for the life of Christ. We no longer live as us, but we now live as Christ on earth.

As Christ-*ians.*

You see, Christ made an exchange for us and with us. He took upon Himself our sin and unrighteousness to save us from eternal separation from God. He then replaced the sin and unrighteousness He took from us with His love and with the power and authority to use His name in the works that we do here on this earth.

With this love and this authority He gave us, we are then to take over the life He lived before being crucified on this cross, the life God called Him to live. We are to do the works God called Him to do. We are to speak the words God called Him to speak. We are to participate in saving the souls God called Him to save. To do these things, we are to love others the way the Father sent Christ to love us.

Let this mind be in you, which was also in Christ Jesus:
Who, being in the form of God, thought it not robbery to be equal with God:
But made himself of no reputation, and took upon him the form of a servant, and was made in the likeness of men:
And being found in fashion as a man, he humbled himself, and became obedient unto death, even the death of the cross.
(Philippians 2:5-8 KJV)

From the moment we become Christians, our minds should be on the things that Christ's mind was on during His human stay here on earth. Why? Because we are here to do what He did, thus we should have the mind He had while doing it. Especially if we desire to be successful at doing it.

In addition, we should do the things Jesus did in Jesus' name and we should do them for the glory of God, not for the glory of self. When we do good, we are doing good in Jesus' name so that God may get the glory for that good and not us. When we love, we are loving so that God may get the glory and not us. When we obey God, we are doing it so that God may get the glory and not us.

We are here living as Christ lived for the purpose Christ lived.

That is what a Christian does and that is who and what a Christian is.

To further understand what a Christian is, we should begin by looking at the suffix "ian".

"ian" means — of, belonging to, relating to, or resembling.

Thus, when you add the letters "ian" to the end of any word, it means something of that word, relating to that word, belonging to that word, and/or resembling that word.

For example, I am a New Orleanian. That means I am of New Orleans, I was born there. I speak the language, my form of dress may resemble the people there. My speech sounds like New Orleans, my behavior is a product of my New Orleans upbringing. In all or some shape, form, or fashion, I represent New Orleans wherever I go.

I am a New Orlean-*ian*.

On the same token, because I represent New Orleans, if I leave my hometown, go somewhere else and do something negative, those who see me and the negativity that is with me are going to relate it to New Orleans. Not just to me.

Just as they did after Hurricane Katrina.

When one or a few New Orleanians did something bad in Houston Texas, all New Orleanians were associated with that negativity and were represented by that negativity even though it was the one or the few who did the negativity.

Thus, when you say you are a Chirst-*ian*, you are claiming to live your life emulating the ways of Christ and you are claiming to live for the reason Christ lived. You are claiming that the way you live, act, and speak is the way Christ lived, acted, and spoke. When you claim to be a Christ*ian*, you are claiming to be an earthly representative of, and an earthly reflection of, Jesus Christ.

How Do We Become Christians?

That if thou shalt confess with thy mouth the Lord Jesus, and shalt believe in thine heart that God hath raised him from the dead, thou shalt be saved.
(Romans 10:9 KJV)

Becoming a Christian according to Romans 10:9 is a two-part process. First, we become Christians by *confessing* Jesus with our mouths and by believing in our hearts that God raised Him from the dead. Thus, in understanding the first part of the process, our first question should be, what then, is the definition of confess?

Well, according to Strong's Exhaustive Concordance, to confess is to **assent**, to **covenant**, to **acknowledge**, to **profess**, to **give thanks**, and to **promise**.

Because Strong's used these words to define confess as it pertains to Romans 10:9 KJV, we are going to look up the definition of each of these words to garner a greater understanding of what it means to confess with our mouths.

So, let's begin with the first word:

<u>Assent</u> – To agree or approve of something.

<u>Covenant</u> – A formal or serious agreement or promise.

<u>Acknowledge</u> – To accept or to *not* deny the truth or existence of something.

<u>Profess</u> – To say or declare something openly.
To say that you are, do, or feel something when other people doubt what you say.
To believe in.

<u>Thank</u> – To express gratitude to someone who has helped you, given something to you, etc.

<u>Promise</u> – A statement telling someone that you will definitely do something or that something will definitely happen.

With these definitions in mind, we now know that to confess Jesus with our mouths means to verbally agree with and approve of Jesus and His existence (***assent***), to verbally agree to follow Jesus and His teachings (**covenant**), to verbally accept and never deny the truth of His existence (***acknowledge***), to declare Jesus and your belief in Him openly even when others doubt Him and you (***profess***), to express gratitude for Jesus and for all He has done for you (**give thanks**), and to tell everyone that you will continue to declare Him, His existence, His marvelous works, and His return (***promise***).

Since the second part of that process is believing in our hearts that God raised Jesus from the dead, our second question should then be what does it mean to believe?

Again, according to Strong's, to believe is to **entrust**, to **commit**, and to put in **trust** with. And again, because Strong's used these words to define *believe*, we are going to look up each of those words to get a greater understanding of what it means to believe according to Romans 10:9 KJV.

The first word we will begin with is:

<u>Entrust</u> – To give someone the responsibility of something, of doing something, or of caring for someone.

<u>Commit</u> – To obligate. To decide to. To put in charge or trust. To put into a place for disposal or for safekeeping.

<u>Trust</u> – Assured reliance on the character, ability, strength, or truth of someone or something.

With these definitions in mind, we now know that to believe, according to Romans 10:9 is to, in your heart, give God the responsibility of having *actually* raised Jesus from the dead (**entrust**), to obligate God to having *actually* raised Jesus from the dead (**commit**), and to have assured reliance on, and faith in, God's character, His ability, and His strength to have miraculously raised Jesus from the dead (**trust**).

After having performed those two parts of the salvation process, you are saved.

It's that simple.

However, as Christians, there is something that we should also understand. We should know and understand that we, Christians, are a people that have accepted the life and the death of Christ. In that death, the blood of Christ was shed. Thus, Christians also accept the blood of Christ knowing that it is that very blood and the acceptance of that shed blood that covers us, that blankets us, that literally makes it so that when God sees us, it is Christ He is actually seeing. That blood is the filter through which God sees us. And when He sees us, the filter of that blood is what causes Him to see us as Christ.

As Christ-*ian*s.

How Do We Behave as Christians?

When Jesus heard it, he saith unto them, They that are whole have no need of the physician, but they that are sick: I came not to call the righteous, but sinners to repentance.
(Mark 2:17 KJV)

Christ came here to call sinners to repentance. Christian behavior is acted out when Christians understand this, when they acknowledge this, and when they do the same as Christ did. After all, that is the purpose of Christianity, being and doing the same as Christ. Spreading the love of God throughout humanity for the saving of souls and for the building of the church. So why is it that so many who claim Christianity bear no reflection of Christ?

The answer to that is two-part and simple.

The first part of that answer is that they don't understand what Christianity is. They have no clue that a Christian is one that believes Christ exchanged and gave His life for theirs and as a result they now exchange and give their life for Christ.

They don't understand that if Christ took upon Himself their sins and unrighteousness, they, in the exchange Christ is offering, should take upon themselves His love and His righteousness. They don't understand the exchange between us and Christ, the switch per se, and as a result they continue being like the world instead of being like Christ.

The second part of this answer is that they are believers, but not followers. Now make no mistake, all Christians are believers, but not all believers are followers of Christ. They believe in Christ, but when it comes to emulating Him, when it comes to being a follower and doer of His teachings, when it comes to being a Christ-*ian*, they have no part in that.

And therein lies a problem.

Christian Behavior vs. non-Christian Behavior

Because you have claimed to be of Christ, because you are claiming to have accepted the exchange that is offered and thus represent Him, you have the power to give Christianity a good, honorable, and morally upstanding reputation. On the opposite side of that same token, you can also reflect Christianity in such a way that you contribute to the reason people look down on it, frown upon it, ridicule it, and reject it.

Why would anyone reflect Christianity in a negative manner?

Because although many of us know that there should be differences in Christian and non-Christian behavior, most have no idea what those differences are or even why those differences exist.

However, there are and should be clear and distinct differences in the behaviors of Christians and non-Christians. And those differences should be such that if a Christian never spoke a word about Christ, their behavior should tell the story of Christ for them.

Why are there differences in behaviors?

Because Christians and non-Christians have two different agendas. Christians are here for God's purpose, non-Christians are here for their own purpose.

<u>Christian Behavior.</u>

One of the reasons a Christian's behavior should be different is because a Christian is a follower of Christ and if Christ came to call sinners away from sin and to repentance, that is what we should be doing as well. But how can we call sinners away from sin and to repentance if we are still sinning and are unrepentant about that sin? And how can we convince anyone that Christ saves and delivers if it appears that He has neither saved us nor delivered us from anything?

The truth of the matter is that we cannot.

We can't convince anyone of anything pertaining to Christ if our behavior gives the impression that we are in bondage to Satan. You see, our behavior can render our Christian ministry completely ineffective if said behavior tells non-Christians that there is no Christ in us. Behaving as a Christian means you must live a life that reflects God, but you cannot and should not live a life that reflects the world.

As we addressed in the beginning of this book, Christians are often told a plethora of things not to do. Don't do this, don't do that. Don't say this, don't say that. Don't wear this, don't wear that. And the list of don'ts seems to go on and on and on. But the list and the reason for the list are rarely and seldomly explained, which is why the list is hated, dreaded, rejected, and oftentimes ignored.

However, the negativity associated with that list does not change the fact that the list is necessary for successful Christianity. And to make the list easier to swallow, try to understand that the list is not exactly a list.

The list is a lifestyle.

And that lifestyle is called Christianity.

In Christianity there are things that we simply cannot do, places we simply cannot be, and characteristics we simply cannot possess or that cannot possess us.

Why?

Because Christians are here to love others, to lead others to Christ. It is for that reason certain behaviors are harmful, not only to us, but also to those we are supposed to love, to those we are supposed to lead to Christ. It is for that reason we should be set apart. Set apart from sin, set apart from worldliness, set apart from unrighteousness.

The main goal of the Christ-like life is love that leads to salvation. Harmful behavior does not exhibit love and in contrast to what we are here for, in contrast to what Christians are called to do, harmful behavior leads to damnation.

Ye are the light of the world. A city that is set on an hill cannot be hid.
Neither do men light a candle, and put it under a bushel, but on a candlestick; and it
giveth light unto all that are in the house.
Let your light so shine before men, that they may see your good works, and glorify your
Father which is in heaven.
(Matthew 5:14-16 KJV)

Being a Christian means that we are a reflection of God's light.

What does light do?

It lights up dark places.

As a Christian, as a reflection of that light, God will usher us into dark places, into the presence of dark people, and into dark situations to shed the light and love of Christ. But how can we shed that light if we are just as dark as the places God sends us to shine His light into? How can we shed that light if we have allowed others to dim our light or to snuff our light out?

The truth is that we cannot.

When we walk into places and notice that there is darkness all around us, that is because we have been assigned to be that light, the light of Christ. However, when we behave no differently than those in the world, all we are doing is spreading darkness everywhere we go instead of shedding God's light everywhere we go.

When we don't behave as Christians should, we are simply adding darkness to places that are already dark, places that may have been in the dark for years. It is for that reason that a Christian's life should *not* be used to indulge in things that have no positive or holy bearing on the church, or in things that have a negative bearing on the church.

We are light and should reflect that light.

Living in such a Godly manner keeps us from falling into things and from getting caught up in things that can hinder our relationship with Christ. It also keeps us separated from those things that can hinder us from leading others to Christ.

That is why we should be set apart. Sanctified. Separated. Holy.

Living a set apart life not only sheds God's light on others, it also protects us from things that are capable of keeping us in bondage for years and years to come. Things like fornication, substance abuse, and idolatry just to name a few. Because if we are distracted by that bondage, fighting that bondage, indulging in that bondage, focused on that bondage, how can we be focused on the souls Christ wants to lead to salvation?

At the same time, being set apart, living a life that does not indulge in worldliness, shows the sinner that they are capable of living a different life while here on earth as well. It reveals that there are those who live in the kingdom of God, those that live under the King's dominion. It shows that we can be in this world and not be *of* this world. It demonstrates the clear and distinct difference between those that belong to Christ and those who do not.

Thus, the list of don'ts serves a purpose that is much deeper than the elders of the church merely stopping us from having "fun". That list is a big part in caring about the condition of the souls of those we are trying to lead to Christ.

And think about this, how bad would we feel if God one day showed us that the ungodly behavior that we displayed is the reason someone fell into a sin so deep they were unable to be, or unwilling to be saved? How would we feel knowing that someone's eternal separation from God was because of our sin and our unrighteousness, sin and unrighteousness we would no longer have if we simply accepted the exchange?

We should also understand that being set apart demonstrates that there is a difference between the dead and the living. The dead are the unsaved. The living are the saved. The dead produces dead fruit or fruit that leads to death. The living produces live fruit or fruit that leads to life.

In this instance, a live person or live fruit would be the one that produces those things which assist in, or lead to, everlasting life. A dead person would be that one that produces what leads to, or assists in, those things that lead to death. And death is eternal separation from God.

For example, a live person would stay away from sin and steer you as far away from sinful and harmful things as is possible. A dead person would live in sin, promote sin, and more likely than not, convince you to sin, oftentimes even participating in that sin with you.

For you to know the difference between who's dead and who's alive, you must know the word of God and that requires diligent study. The word of God is alive, it teaches you how to be alive, thus, knowing it and obeying it is a crucial matter of life and death.

Not just for you, but for others as well.

However, if you do not study the word, you are susceptible and vulnerable to the dead and to those things that can and will bring about not only the death of the sinner, but your own death as well.

Thus, the separation.

Thus, being set apart.

Thus, the infamous list of don'ts.

What We Should Understand.

We should understand that when we claim to be Christian, we are claiming to look like Christ, live like Christ, sound like Christ, and obey God as did Christ. We are claiming that our lives are our ministry and that we will use our lives, our ministry, to draw sinners to repentance just as Christ did. We are claiming to live lives that serve a Godly purpose. Not a fleshly purpose, not a selfish purpose, but a Godly purpose.

And because we are representatives of Christ, whether we are representing Christ accurately or not, to those who do not know Him, when they see one who is claiming to be a Christian, they believe they are seeing a reflection of Christ. Therefore, when they see us, they are seeing Christ. When they hear us speak, they are hearing Christ speak. When we move, they are seeing Christ move. Our actions tell them what Christ did. Our lives tell them who Christ was. Our words tell them what Christ said.

Therefore, if we are reflecting Christ as worldly, how can they believe that a worldly man was capable of living a sin free life, of being crucified, and then of being raised from the dead to save our souls?

The truth is that they can't believe it.

Why can't they?

Because they know and truly believe that if *they* are worldly and *they* can't do it, then neither can any other worldly person do it. And that makes them question whether or not the worldly Christ you're showing them is capable of doing it as well. In addition, their questioning how, if they have no desire to do it in their worldly state, could a worldly Christ even *bother* to do it.

If we don't possess so minute a power as to reflect Christ correctly, so minute a power as to live as if we are saved, they won't believe that Christ saved us. And in turn, how can they then believe Christ had and has so great a power as to actually save *their* unsaved souls?

Our actions reflect Christ's love.

Our actions reflect Christ's power.

Thus, our lives, the way we live, should make them not only know that Christ did it, but that Christ can also do it through them. Therefore, being Christian means being an accurate reflection of Christ so much so, that the world trusts and believes that Christ not only lived back then, but that He is still alive today.

Alive and still saving souls.

It is from this we learn that as Christians we really only have two options, live lives that reflect Christ or live lives that reflect death. Live lives that assist in the saving of souls or be active participants in the eternal separation of souls from God.

Those who are Christ-*ian* light the path to Christ for those that are living in darkness, and our separated and sanctified behavior should reflect that.

Why Should We Be Christians?

First, we should be Christians because God loves us, genuinely loves us, and does not want us to perish. Without Christ we are guaranteed to perish. Second, we should be Christians because Christianity restores us to the original condition God created us to be in, a condition that put us at one with Him for eternity. And lastly, we should be Christians because as Christians we can lead many others to Christ as well.

Is that a big responsibility? Yes. But as those who are on a mission of love, as those of us who are called to love, it is not a responsibility that we should be unwilling to take on.

Why?

Because as Christians, we may be the only way in which some people ever see Christ. We may be the only bible some people will ever read.

In simpler terms, being a Christian means three things. It means that we are a living manifestation of the *word* of God. We are also a living manifestation of Christ who is the living manifestation of God. And lastly, just as Christ is the physical embodiment of God, we are the physical embodiment of Jesus Christ.

Therefore, the way we live should reveal as much.

~

Section Two

~

CHAPTER FIVE

Christianity Requires a Relationship with God.

Behold, I stand at the door, and knock: if any man hear my voice, and open the door, I will come in to him, and will sup with him, and he with me.
(Revelation 3:20 KJV)

As we go farther in our Christianity, it is of the utmost importance that we have a relationship with God. After all, this is the God we have elected to believe in, and this is the God we have chosen to serve. With that being said, how can we be effective as Christians if we know not the God we serve?

Simply put, we can't.

Not only can we not be effective in our own Christianity if we don't know God, we can be downright harmful to the Christianity of others. And how can we not have a relationship with God when Jesus, the One we follow, has an ongoing relationship with the Father?

Again, we cannot.

It is for this reason that we should have a deep, personal, and close relationship with the One we have chosen to place our faith in. Therefore, to begin this journey, the question we should ask is:

What Is a Relationship with God?

The word relationship is defined as the way in which two or more people or things are **connected** or **interrelated**.

<u>Connected</u> - Joined or linked together.

<u>Interrelated</u> - Having a mutual or **reciprocal relation**.

<u>Reciprocal</u> – Shared, felt, or shown by both sides.

<u>Relation</u> - The way in which two or more people, groups, countries, etc., talk to, behave toward, and deal with each other.
The way in which two or more people or things are connected.
A person who is a member of your family.

Based on those definitions, we can clearly see that a relationship is the way in which we connect. It is a reciprocal joining together with, and a reciprocal relating to, one another. In Christianity, the joining together, the relating to, and the connecting with would be with God. The fact that the relationship with God is reciprocal tells us that not only are we doing things for God and for the church, but God is also doing things for us.
Christianity is not a one-way street.
It is a healthy, reciprocal *relation*ship with God.

How to Have a Relationship with God.

When in a healthy relationship, we do things to ensure that our mate is happy. We talk to them, yes, because verbal communication is very important, but we also listen to them. We learn their likes and dislikes, we learn what hurts them and what heals them. We learn what turns them off and what motivates them. We learn their goals, dreams, visions and aspirations, and we strive to do those things that *please* them and to *help* them with their dreams as much as we can.
Why do we do this?
Because we love them.

Well, the same love should apply to God in our relationship with Him. We should learn those things that He likes and strive to do them. When He asks us to do something, we should immediately do what He asks of us, trusting that as the Creator, as One who is omniscient, He knows what is best for us and for those around us.

So how do we have a relationship with God?

We communicate with Him.

However, communication is not just verbal, there is action involved and that action speaks volumes. There's a saying that goes, "Action speaks louder than words." In Christianity, there are some instances when that is the case, when much more is required than just lip service. Thus, in the following chapters we're going to list the actions that are required for a healthy relationship with God.

Why Should We Have a Relationship with God?

We should have a relationship with God to be effective as Christians. After all, we have agreed to be demonstrations of His love here on earth, we have agreed to be followers of Christ, and we have agreed to love God's people. However, how can we do any of these things if we have no relationship with the God we have agreed to do these things with?

Simply put, we can't.

Thus, to be effective in your relationship with God, there are certain things you *must* do. There are things that are required of you to be a good and effective Christian, things that would make your mission easier, and things that would draw you closer and closer to the God you are in a relationship with in every passing day.

What are those things?

Well, you must have faith.

You must pray.

You must study.

You must commit.

And you must surrender.

Are any of these things easy to do or have? No. However, they are all necessary, very necessary for the ministry you have become a part of. They are necessary to relate to God and they are necessary for the saving of souls.

So, let us begin where it all begins.

With a little something called faith.

CHAPTER SIX

Christianity Requires Faith

But without faith it is impossible to please him: for he that cometh to God must believe that he is, and that he is a rewarder of them that diligently seek him.
(Hebrews 11:6 KJV)

Before anyone can be a Christian, they must have faith, a belief in God, a belief that God exists, a belief that God is who He says He is, a belief that He has done what He says He has done, and a belief that He can and will do what He says He can and will do.

Why?

Because at the root of Christianity is faith. And you can't have Christianity if you don't have faith.

What Is Faith?

Now faith is the substance of things hoped for, the evidence of things not seen.
(Hebrews 11:1 KJV)

Many of us have either read or heard that scripture a million times and yet have no idea what it really means. We have gone years quoting it but have been unable to apply it to our lives because we are not aware of its significance, let alone the depth of the role faith plays in our Christianity. Therefore, to come to a better understanding of this scripture, and to better apply it to our lives and to our Christianity, let's take the time to study it.

Faith.

As it is used in Hebrews 11:1, Faith, according to Strong's is defined as **credit**, to **entrust** (especially one's spirituality to Christ), **believe, commit,** put in **trust** with.

To fully understand what the definition of faith is, we should look up every word Strong's gave as a definition, beginning with the first word.

<u>Credit</u> – Reliance on the truth or reality of something.
A record of how well you have paid or done something in the past.
Credibility.
A source of honor.

<u>Believe</u> – To accept or regard something as true.
To accept the truth of what is said.

<u>Commit</u> – To say that something or someone will definitely do something.
To make someone or something obligated to do something.

<u>Trust</u> – Belief that something or someone is good, honest, reliable, effective, etc.
Assured reliance on the ability, character, strength, or truth of someone or something.
Something committed or entrusted to someone to be used or cared for in the interest of another.

Substance, as it was originally written in Greek, means a setting under (**support**), **essence, assurance, confidence, substance**.
To better understand those words, let's define them further.

<u>Support</u> – Assistance or help to hold up or serve as a **foundation**.
To keep something going.
To endure.

<u>**Foundation**</u> – Usually a stone or concrete structure that supports
       a building from underneath.
       Something that provides support for something.
       An underlying base or support.
       A body or ground upon which something is built
       or overlaid.
       The support upon which something rests.
       The act of beginning or creating.

<u>**Substance**</u> - **Ultimate reality** that **underlies** all **manifestations**.
       (Physical) material from which something is made or
       which has discrete existence.

<u>**Ultimate**</u> - Happening or coming at the end of a process or series
       of events.

<u>**Reality**</u> - Something that actually exists or happens.
       A real event, occurrence, situation, etc.

<u>**Underlies**</u> - To be at the basis of.
       Form the foundation of.

<u>**Manifestation**</u> - A perceptible, outward, or visible expression of
       something.

<u>**Evidence**</u>, according to Strong's, means **proof, conviction, reproof.**
To garner a greater understanding let's look those definitions up.

<u>**Proof**</u> – something which shows that something else is true or
       correct.
       An act or process of showing that something else is true.
       Something that induces certainty or establishes validity.
       A photographic print made from a negative.

<u>**Conviction**</u> – A strong belief or opinion.
       The feeling of being sure that what you believe or say
       is true.
       The state of being convinced.

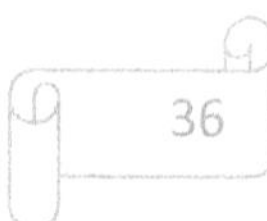

<u>**Reproof**</u> – **Blame** or criticism for a fault.

<u>**Blame**</u> - To say or think that a person or thing is responsible for something that happened.
To hold responsible.

From these defined words we can gather that Hebrews 11:1 means that reliance on the truth or reality of what we hope for (**faith**) is the act of beginning or creating (**substance**) what we hope for and, the proof (**evidence**) of what we hope for, which is those things we cannot yet see. However, we're going to take this further and look at faith in laymen's terms. We're going to look at faith from a deeper and different perspective.

Faith.

Let's look at faith from the perspective of building a house.

Now we know that when building a house, a foundation has to be laid. What is a foundation? A foundation is the weight that holds the house up and that holds the house together. The foundation is what supports the weight of the house. If there is no foundation, the house has nothing to support it and nothing to stand on. With nothing supporting it, the first time a good wind blows, the house will fall.

Thus, in building this house, not just any foundation can be laid, only a foundation that is strong enough to support the house that is being built on top of it can be laid. If the house weighs ten thousand pounds, you cannot build a foundation for that house that is only capable of holding three thousand pounds. If you do that, the very foundation of the house will collapse under the pressure of the weight of the house. Therefore, if the foundation is weak, the house will fall because the foundation is not strong enough to support what is sitting on top of it.

If the foundation isn't strong, neither is what is built on top of that foundation.

Why?

Because what you build is only as strong as its foundation, only as strong as what supports it, only as strong as what holds it up.

In Christianity, your foundation is your faith. If you don't believe in God, you have no faith in God. Without faith in God, you have no foundation in God. If you don't believe in Christ, you have no faith in Christ. Without faith in Christ, you have no foundation in Christ. And without a foundation in Christ, you have no Christianity. Thus, your faith in

God is the very foundation upon which the entirety of your Christianity is built.

Now, let's say that you have a strong foundation in God. Since we know that your foundation is your faith, that means that your foundation is strong enough for God to build on.

Build what?

Strong enough to build whatever your foundation can hold.

Strong enough to build whatever your faith can support.

Your faith would be strong enough to build a strong Christianity on. There will be things in Christianity and in life that you can handle that others may not be able to. This is not because you are better, not because you love God more, not even because God loves you more. You will be able to handle more because your foundation can hold more.

It's that simple.

Thus, whatever you are believing God for, your faith is the substance, the essence, the heart of that belief. Once your foundation is laid, God can build anything on top of that faith that your faith can hold. Because our faith is the foundation, God is the builder, and what we hope for is what is being built.

On the flip side of that coin, God can also build anything on top of your faith that your foundation cannot hold. But do you really want Him to? Because whatever He builds on a weak foundation *will* fall and it will fall because the weight of what is built is too heavy for the foundation it is built upon. For that reason, a strong foundation is needed in Christianity.

But where does a strong foundation come from?

A strong foundation comes from God. It comes from spending time with Him, time in His word. It comes from spending time with Him in prayer. It comes from spending time with Him in praise.

The more time and dedication you give God, the more you see Him in your everyday life and in your everyday walk with Him. The more you see God, the more you see what He does, what He has done, and what He is capable of doing. The more you see what he has done and what He is capable of doing, the more you begin to trust Him with the things you need done. And before you know it, without you even realizing it, God has developed a reliable and unshakeable track record with you.

That is when you begin to trust Him.

The more you trust God, the greater your foundation in God. The greater your foundation in God, your faith in God, the greater that which God builds upon your foundation will be.

Your faith also holds the materials needed to build what you are believing God to build. Therefore, if you are believing God for marriage and marriage requires love, your relationship with God, your dedication to God, your faith in God determines just how much of God's love you have allowed Him to fill you with. Your service to God determines how much service you will be able to give your spouse. Your loyalty to God determines how much loyalty you will be able to give your significant other. Everything needed for a successful marriage in Christ is directly determined by the closeness of your relationship with God.

With all of that being said, according to Hebrews 11:1 your faith is the foundation that supports and gets God to build what you hope for. And the fact that you have that faith is evidence that what you have faith in really does exist even though you cannot see it.

What We Should Have Faith In?

Our faith should always be in God.

You see, the faith we have, the foundation we have, should never be in the *thing* we are believing God for, but in the very **God** that creates the thing we are believing God for. For instance, if we are believing God for marriage but our faith is in marriage, then our marriage is only as strong as marriage is, not as strong as God, the One who creates and builds the marriage. Thus, our faith should always be in God's ability to manifest the thing, not in the thing's ability to manifest itself.

Why?

Because the thing can neither build nor support itself, but God can both build and support the thing.

In addition, what sense does it make to have faith in the creation and not in the Creator? Is the creation greater than the Creator? Can the creation do or be anything without the power of God?

No.

Who changed the truth of God into a lie, and worshipped and served the creature more than the Creator, who is blessed for ever. Amen.
(Romans 1:25 KJV)

Thus, why would we have faith in anything or anyone other than God?

Now, am I saying that we should never have faith in people? No. What I am saying is that we should have faith in God, in God's ability to work things through and in people. And if we were to really think about faith and what faith is, we would have to question why God would lead us to have more faith in things and more faith in people than we have in Him, the creator of those things.

For example, if your faith was in money, and you believed that money could and would get you everything your heart desired, why would you need God? After all, your belief would be that money does everything for you, *everything*. So, what purpose would God serve in your life? To you, because of your faith in money, God would not be needed because money serves your every purpose. Thus, for you, there would be no need to believe in Him or to serve Him.

The same goes for having faith in self. If you believed that you were the master of your fate, if you believed that you were your own god and any and everything you needed was in you, came through you, and was only manifested by you, why would you need God? The truth of the matter is that you would truly believe you didn't need God. You'd believe that all you needed was you, thereby making God of none effect in your life. Until you came upon a situation that you realized was greater than you and greater than what you could handle.

Like eternal salvation.

You see, the money you would believe in could not buy your salvation and the belief you would have in yourself could not save your soul. And if you were to try and enter into eternity with your money and with yourself as your own god, you would quickly come to the realization that the only eternity you're going to get in with all of your money and all of your own might is the eternity that comes with damnation. Not the eternity that comes with salvation.

Why?

Because you and money can't save your soul.

Only Jesus can do that.

And the only way to get to the Father, which is in eternity, is through Jesus.

Not through money.

And not through self.

Jesus saith unto him, I am the way, the truth, and the life: no man cometh unto the Father, but by me.

Thus, when you exhausted all of your own power and all of money's ability, then and only then would you see and know the need for God.

That is why scripture tells us to have faith and to have faith in God.

Now in the morning as he returned into the city, he hungered.
And when he saw a fig tree in the way, he came to it, and found nothing thereon, but leaves only, and said unto it, Let no fruit grow on thee henceforward for ever. And presently the fig tree withered away. And when the disciples saw it, they marvelled, saying, How soon is the fig tree withered away!
Jesus answered and said unto them, Verily I say unto you, If ye have faith, and doubt not, ye shall not only do this which is done to the fig tree, but also if ye shall say unto this mountain, Be thou removed, and be thou cast into the sea; it shall be done.
(Matthew 21:18-21)

Who was Jesus telling them to have faith in?

And Jesus answering saith unto them, Have faith in God.
(Mark 11:22 KJV)

Why was Jesus telling them to have faith in God?

Because what Jesus was able to do to the fig tree came from his faith in His Father. It came from His Father's ability to turn His words, His wishes, and His desires into reality through Himself.

Thus, in this instance, Jesus was trusting that God would use Him as the instrument through which God Himself would both build and destroy something. God used Jesus' words and Jesus' desire for the fig tree to be cursed to destroy the fig tree's ability to produce. On the same token, God also used Jesus' words and the destruction of the fig tree's ability to produce to add to the disciples' foundation of faith in God. Because by seeing what God did through Jesus, the faith the disciples had in God's ability to use them as He did Jesus was strengthened.

It is for this reason that your faith should never be in yourself, but in God and in God's ability to use you, to work in you, and to work thorough you.

Your faith should always be in God.

With all of that being said, we should know that when it comes to faith God never expects us to have blind faith. Especially since God has been demonstrating who He is and what He is capable of since the foundation of the earth.

You see, God created the world, and in that act, He has proven that He can do any and everything He wills to do. God created mankind, again proving the power of what He can and will do. God created you and the domino effect of things it takes to keep you, your mind, your body, and your spirit all working and alive. That in and of itself is miraculous and a demonstration of what He can and will do. Therefore, your faith in God is never blind.

In fact, your faith in God comes from merely looking around and seeing His capabilities and His power. Not only that, but there have been things that each of us have prayed for from God and have received. There have been things that we have not prayed for from God and yet we still received them. In doing these things, giving us these things, blessing us with these things, God has laid a foundation of trust that you can and should have in Him. And if we are paying attention, we can see these things clearly and know that any future faith we have in Him, or may be required to have in Him, is not and never will be blind. Unlike Thomas who doubted not only that the disciples had seen Jesus, but also that God had raised Jesus from the dead, we do not need further proof to believe.

Thomas needed proof that Jesus had indeed been risen. However, everything Jesus had done while in the presence of the disciples, of which Thomas was one, should have been demonstration enough for Thomas that Jesus had indeed risen on the third day. Everything God had done prior to Thomas knowing Jesus should have been proof enough that God did indeed possess the power to raise Jesus from the dead. The fact that God, through Jesus, raised Lazarus from the dead should have been proof positive that God was perfectly capable of raising Jesus the same way. And finally, the fact that Jesus, who is not only the Son of the living God, but God Himself, should have been proof for Thomas that God had indeed raised Jesus from the dead.

Thomas saith unto him, Lord, we know not whither thou goest;
and how can we know the way?
Jesus saith unto him, I am the way, the truth, and the life:
no man cometh unto the Father, but by me.
If ye had known me, ye should have known my Father also:

It is for those reasons that we have our faith and our trust not in things, not in mankind, and not in self, but in God and in God's abilities to do what He needs to do in and through us all.

Why Should We Have Faith?

We should have faith simply because…

Without faith we can't have Christ.
Without Christ we can't have salvation.
Without salvation we can't have God.
And without God we can't help anyone, including ourselves.

CHAPTER SEVEN

Christianity Requires Prayer

And it came to pass in those days, that he went out into a mountain to pray, and continued all night in prayer to God.
(Luke 6:12 KJV)

At some point in our walk with God we are going to have to engage in a conversation with Him. We are going to have to listen to God. We are going to have to obey God. However, we can't do any of those things if we can't hear what He commands, if we can't hear Him talking, or if we don't know the sound of His voice when He does talk.

So how do we know what God's commandments are? How do we hear Him talking? How do we know His voice?

Simply put, we have conversations with Him

Okay, but how do we have a conversation with God?

Even more simple, we pray.

Because the first and most important way that we develop and have a relationship with God is through prayer, through continual conversations with Him.

What Is Prayer?

In a nutshell, prayer is communication with and to God.

However, for a more in depth definition of prayer, we must know what prayer is according to Luke 6:12. So let's define prayer.

According to Luke chapter six the word pray means to _**supplicate**_ to God and to _**worship**_.

Since the first word we have as a definition of pray is supplicate, we are going to define the word supplicate.

**Supplicate** – To make a humble entreaty; especially : to pray to God.
                    To ask earnestly and humbly. **Beseech. Implore. Beg. Entreat. Plead.**

Because the definition of the word **_supplicate_** gave us many synonyms, we are going to define each of these synonyms to garner a deeper understanding.

Beseech – To beg (someone) for something: to ask (someone) in
                    a serious and emotional way to do something.

Implore – To make a very serious or emotional request to someone.

Beg –To ask someone in a very serious and emotional way for
                    something needed or wanted very much.

Entreat - To plead with especially in order to persuade.

Plead - To ask for something in a serious and emotional way.

Now that we have defined the word supplicate, we are going to define **worship** which is another word used in the definition of pray.

**Worship** – _**Reverence**_ toward a divine being or supernatural power. _**Extravagant respect**_ or _**admiration**_ or _**devotion**_.

Reverence - Honor or respect that is felt for or shown to
                    someone or something.

Extravagant - Exceeding the limits of reason or necessity.
                    Lacking in moderation, balance, and restraint.
                    Extremely or excessively elaborate.

<u>Respect</u> - A feeling or understanding that someone or something is important, serious, etc., and should be treated in an appropriate way.

<u>Admiration</u> - A feeling of great respect and approval.

<u>Devotion</u> - A feeling of strong love or loyalty to someone or something.

Based on the definition of pray and all of its synonyms, to pray is to go to God, to communicate with God, or to ask God for something humbly, seriously, and in an emotional manner. To worship God is to exceedingly, excessively, and elaborately respect, honor, admire, and reverence God. With all of those definitions in mind, we know that according to Luke chapter six and verse twelve we are to communicate with God and worship Him.

After all, if Jesus did it, if Jesus worshipped God, how can *we* not?

However, to stress the importance of this type of communication, let's look at it from a more natural and a somewhat easier to understand standpoint. Let's view that communication through something the majority of us are familiar with.

Relationships.

In relationships couples communicate. In successful relationships, they communicate well. Therefore, just as couples communicate in relationships to keep the relationship healthy, loving, and long lasting, we are going to have to communicate with God. After all, we are in a relationship with God. We are doing what God called us to do while oftentimes asking Him to do things for us. Thus, we must communicate with Him if we expect to have a healthy, loving, and long lasting relationship with Him.

We must communicate with Him spiritually.

Mentally.

Emotionally.

And physically.

But first we must communicate with Him verbally and that verbal communication is called prayer.

What Should We Pray?

There are so many things we should pray that it would be impossible to list them all. However, there are some basics that every Christian should pray daily, basics we learned from Jesus.

After this manner therefore pray ye: Our Father which art in heaven, Hallowed be thy name.
Thy kingdom come, Thy will be done in earth, as it is in heaven.
Give us this day our daily bread.
And forgive us our debts, as we forgive our debtors.
And lead us not into temptation, but deliver us from evil: For thine is the kingdom, and the power, and the glory, for ever. Amen.
(Matthew 6:9-13 KJV)

Based on this example that Jesus gave us, the first thing we should do when we pray is acknowledge God, the Father, the One to whom we are speaking. This acknowledgement is done when we say, "Our Father."

However, not only are we acknowledging the Father, Our Father, but we are also acknowledging that the Father of which we speak is in Heaven. This acknowledgement makes it clear which God Christians are praying to and separates them from those praying to false gods.

Furthermore, we say, "Our." The word our means we are not only talking to God about ourselves, but that we are talking to Him about others as well. It establishes that although this is an intimate prayer, it is not a self-seeking prayer. It is not only about us, just as Christianity is not *only* about us. Instead, this particular prayer is about the church as a whole, just as our Christianity should be.

The next thing we are to do in prayer is to acknowledge the holiness of God, the very fact that He is set apart from everything else and from every other god. This is done when we say the words, "Hallowed be they name."

The word **Hallowed** means holy, purify, consecrate, venerate, sanctify.

<u>Holy</u> - Exalted or worthy of complete devotion as one perfect in goodness and righteousness.

<u>Purify</u> – To make pure.
To free from guilt or moral or ceremonial blemish.
To free from undesirable elements.

<u>**Consecrate**</u> – To make or declare sacred.

<u>**Venerate**</u> - To feel or show deep respect for someone or something that is considered great, holy, etc.

<u>**Sanctify**</u> - To set apart to a sacred purpose or to religious use. To impart or impute sacredness, inviolability, or respect to.

Based on the definition of Hallowed, and the synonyms given with that definition, we now know that saying, "Hallowed be they name," to God in prayer, is an affirmation of God's holiness and His perfection. It is a verbal declaration of your belief in God's holiness, in His perfection, in the excellence of His name.

The next words out of our mouths in this prayer is, "Thy Kingdom come." For the meaning of this to be explained it must first be explained what a kingdom is.

<u>Kingdom</u> – Rule, a realm, kingdom, reign.

<u>**Rule**</u> – The exercise of authority or control. The period during which someone or something exercises authority or control. To have control and power over a country, area, group, etc.

<u>**Realm**</u> – **Sphere** or **domain**.

<u>**Sphere**</u> – An area or range over or within which someone or something acts, exists, or has influence or significance.

<u>**Domain**</u> – The land that a ruler or governor controls. A territory over which dominion is exercised.

<u>**Kingdom**</u> – A country whose ruler is a king or queen. The spiritual world in which God is king. The realm in which God's will is fulfilled. A realm or region in which something is dominant. An area or sphere in which one holds a preeminent position.

Reign – A royal authority.
> The dominion, sway, or influence of one resembling a
> monarch.
> The time during which one reigns.
> To possess or exercise sovereign power.
> The period of time during which a king, queen, emperor, etc.,
> is a ruler of a country.

With all of these definitions in mind we should understand that when praying the words, "Thy kingdom come," we are asking God to let His holy reign, His holy dominion, His holy authority, His sovereign power come to where we are and rule.

By praying for this, we are also acknowledging that we want to be under God's rule, under His holy dominion, and that we are ready to willfully surrender to His dominion as citizens of His kingdom, the kingdom that we are asking to come. And if we are not ready to submit to His will, to be under His authority, under His reign, under His rule, then why are we asking for His kingdom to come?

The next words, "Thy will be done in earth as it is in Heaven," are asking God to let His will, His wants, His desires be done, completed, obeyed, and acted out in earth the same way His will is desired, done, completed, obeyed, and acted out in Heaven. We are acknowledging that we want to do what God wills us to do here in earth. We are acknowledging that we want to follow *His* leadership and *His* vision, not our own and not the world's.

"Give us this day our daily bread," is saying that we want God to supply our needs *today*. However, we are not just asking God to supply us with bread as in food, we are asking Him to supply us with whatever we need to do what He wills. Bread as in the bread of life, bread as in whatever is needed to sustain us and to help us sustain others *that day*.

However, why do we ask for God's sustenance daily instead of once and for all? Because asking daily keeps us in communication with Him daily. Asking God to give us these things once and forever means we never have to go to Him for anything again, and that would mean a life without prayer, a life without communication with God.

Since God understands that we need to talk to Him more than once in life, and since He wants to talk to us more than once in life, He directed us to come to Him daily. Therefore, we ask Him only for what we need daily, giving us the chance and the need to speak to Him each and every day we live.

And what do we ask Him for each and every day?

We are asking for our daily dose of His wisdom, our daily dose of His love, of His mercy, of His kindness. We are asking for our daily dose of his guidance, of his counsel, and of his leadership. And we are asking not just for daily bread for ourselves, but for others as well. That is why we say, "Give *us*," and not "Give me."

"And forgive us our **debts** as we forgive our **debtors**," are the next words in the prayer.

The definition of the word **debts** in this scripture is – Something **owed**, a **moral fault**.

Owe – A need to repay.
> To do something or to give something to someone who has done something for you or given something to you.

Moral – Concerning or relating to what is right and wrong in human behavior.

Fault – A bad quality or part of someone's character.
> A problem or bad part that prevents something from being perfect.
> A flaw or defect.
> Responsibility for a problem, mistake, or bad situation, etc.

Debtor – A person who owes a debt.

With the definition of, and synonyms of, debt and debtor in mind, we now know that when asking God to forgive us our debts, we are asking Him to forgive us of our faults, our sins, our bad qualities, our flaws, our defects, our imperfections. We are asking Him to forgive us of the problems, mistakes, and bad decisions we are responsible for. We are asking Him to forgive us of the sinful debts we have committed against others and ultimately against Him.

On the opposite side of that forgiveness, we are also asking God to forgive us just as we forgive our debtors, as we forgive those we feel have sinned and transgressed against us. We are asking God to use the same measure of forgiveness on us that we use on others. If we forgive others very little, then we are asking God to forgive us very little. If we forgive much, then we are asking God to forgive us very much. After all, the words we are saying are, "Forgive us our debts *as* we forgive our debtors," and the word **as** means to the same degree or amount.

Then next part of the prayer is, "And lead us not into temptation."

When taking a deeper look at the word temptation, we see that its definition, as used in the Bible, means **experience of evil, solicitation, discipline** or **provocation, adversity, temptation, try**.

<u>**Experience**</u> – The process of doing and seeing things and having things happen to you.
Something personally encountered, undergone, or lived through.
To feel or be affected by something.
To have experience of.
The process of living through an event or events.
To undergo or live through.

<u>**Evil**</u> – Morally bad or reprehensible.
Causing harm or injury to someone.
Tending to injure.
Something that brings sorrow, trouble, hardship, or destruction.

<u>**Solicitation**</u> – The practice or an act or instance of soliciting.
Incitement or allurement.

<u>**Discipline**</u> - Punishment.
Training that corrects, molds, or perfects the mental faculties or moral character.
To punish as a way to bring about good behavior.

<u>**Provocation**</u> – The act or process of **provoking**.

<u>**Provoke**</u> – To cause a person to become angry or violent.
Something that causes anger or (sometimes negative) action.

<u>**Adversity**</u> – A difficult situation or tragedy.
           Misfortune or tragedy.
           Hard times.

<u>**Try**</u> – To put to test or trial.
           To subject to something (as undue strain or excessive hardship or provocation) that tests the powers of endurance.

<u>**Temptation**</u> – A strong urge or desire to have or do something, especially something that is bad or wrong or unwise.

With this verse of prayer, we must understand that the first definition of the biblical word temptation is an *experience of evil.* Thus, it stands to reason that every word that follows pertains to evil. In this instance we would be asking God to keep us away from all evil experiences. We would be asking Him to keep us away from all evil solicitations, away from anything or anyone that would solicit us or incite us to do evil.

We are asking God to keep us away from any type of discipline or punishment that is evil, that serves no Godly purpose, but instead is designed to hurt or corrupt us or others. We are asking God to keep us away from anything that would provoke us to be evil or do evil, or speak evil, or think evil. We are asking our Father to lead us away from, in the opposite direction of, any evil adversity, any evil test or trial and/or any evil temptation.

That is why we say the words, "And lead us *not* into temptation."

That is also why we say the words, "But deliver us from evil." Because we are asking God not to *lead* us into any evil places or situations, but instead to *deliver* us from them.

The word deliver, by definition, means to save someone or something from danger or harm. Thus, we are asking to be led nowhere near evil, hurt, harm, or danger, but to be saved and spared from it all.

"For thine is the kingdom and the power and the glory, forever."

Here is where we're going to be very technical with our words. In this particular instance "**For**" is a function word that means *because.*

Now, to understand the next word which is, "Thine," we must look at the word **thine**. Thine is an archaic Greek word that means *thine own,* which would let us know that something that is *thine own* is something that belongs to you, something that *you own.* The *you* in this case would be God the Father, to whom we are praying. Thus, when we say, "**For thine**," we are really saying, "Because yours (God's) is…"

"The Kingdom, the power, and the glory, forever." What we are saying in this part of the prayer is that the kingdom belongs to God, the power belongs to God, and the glory belongs to God forever.

But what exactly is the kingdom, the power, and the glory?

Well, we have already established that the kingdom is God's rule, His reign, and His dominion. The **power** is miraculous power, ability, abundance, might, mighty work. And the glory is, dignity, honor, praise, worship.

Therefore, we can only pray to God for the kingdom to come because the kingdom belongs to Him. We can only pray to God to do the things we ask because He alone possesses the miraculous power, the ability, the abundance and the might to do the mighty works which we are asking. And we can only pray to God for the help to remain in His will so that only He may get the glory from our lives just as He did with Jesus, the glory that belongs to Him anyway.

And all of this belongs to God forever, meaning without end and never ceasing.

The final word we say in this prayer is, "**Amen**," which means *so be it*.

Now let's break this down as far as we can break it down to get the best understanding possible. The definition of the word **so** is *therefore or most certainly, or without doubt*. The word **be** in this instance is a verb and that particular verb is defined as *exist or live*. In this instance **it** is a pronoun that is defined as *the thing, act, or matter about which these words are spoken or written*.

Therefore, when we are done praying to our Father, we are ending that prayer with a single word that means, *therefore, most definitely, and without doubt the things, acts, and matters of which we have just spoken lives and exists*. That one word is an expression of our faith. It is a word that declares to God our unwavering belief in His ability and in His will to bring what we have petitioned from Him to pass. It is an affirmation that says we know our petitions have been heard and that because everything is His, God's, we know that the manifestation of our prayers exist *right now*!

What a powerful way to end a prayer.

A prayer that Jesus used to teach us what to pray.

When Should We Pray?

Why should we pray nonstop, why should we pray without ceasing? The answer to that is simple.

To remain in constant spiritual connection with God.

You see, the days we live here on Earth are spent surrounded by that which is carnal. Be it people, music, movies, work, school, books, television, or life in general, we are often subjected to and exposed to some things that are seriously spiritually deficient.

While we are surrounded by that which is spiritually deficient, a lot of our focus has to be on that which is spiritually deficient and as a result we can easily become distracted by that which is spiritually deficient.

Now by definition, the word distraction means something that makes it difficult to think or pay attention. The world is for some, and can be for many, one big distraction. As Christians we are not supposed to be thinking about, or paying attention to, worldly things. We are supposed to be thinking about and paying attention to spiritual things. A distraction can make it difficult to think about, pay attention to, or focus on the things of God.

In the midst of that distraction, and depending on the length of that distraction, we can become connected to that distraction. Instead of our focus being temporarily on the worldly, it can become extensively focused on the carnal or the worldly. And once we connect to the carnal, we run the risk of becoming disconnected from the spiritual.

To prevent this disconnect from happening, we should pray without ceasing. Prayer keeps us constantly connected to God, it keeps us connected even in the midst of worldliness and carnality. And that connection, that never ending connection, allows us to be *in* the world, without becoming **of** the world.

Of – belonging to, relating to, or connected with (someone or something).

As Christians we may be here in this world, but we do not belong to the world, we do not relate to the world, and we are not connected with the world. We are here on a Godly mission, a mission that requires us to remain

in constant connection with God. Thus, the need for praying without ceasing.

Now, does constant prayer mean we must be on our knees, bowed down before God twenty-four-seven? Not unless we're on some kind of fast that requires such action. However, just because we are not on our knees all of the time does not mean we can't pray in our heads and in our hearts without ceasing.

We should also know that the word pray in 1st Thessalonians 5:17 means to worship, supplicate, to pray. Worship is a form of prayer and thus, we can worship God all day every day. We can worship Him with praise. We can worship Him with song. We can worship Him with dance. Just because we are not praying in one sense does not mean we cannot pray in another.

No matter how we pray, however, we should do it without ceasing.

Why We Should Pray?

We should pray because communicating with the God of which we serve is a crucial part of our Christianity. We cannot be effective in our walk with God if we do not talk to Him. We need to talk to God for His instruction, to know what He requires of us in each individual situation of our lives. We need to talk to God for His leadership because who is there better than Him to lead us in this walk with Him? We need to talk to God for His guidance, guidance that will enable us to live the life He gave us the way in which He gave it to us to live.

We should pray to keep in constant contact with God, especially since we are in a world where so many are going against God and have no contact with Him at all. We should pray for peace in a world where chaos seems to be everywhere. We should pray for understanding, to understand the God we serve, to understand the world He placed us in to live, to understand His word, to understand His instruction, and to understand Christianity.

We should pray for God's protection from those who mean us harm. We should pray for the salvation of all. We should pray that everyone comes to know Christ. And we should pray because plenty of others need us to petition God on their behalf whether they, or we, know it or not.

We should pray because there is a world full of people that are dying. They are dying spiritually, emotionally, mentally and physically. They are dying because they are in need of God, but they can't see Him because they are too busy being blinded by others and the need others have to be seen. They can't see that they are dying because they are too busy living for and in this world instead of living for God in this world. They are dying, being separated from God daily, and they have no idea.

There are so many reasons why we should pray, but at the end of the day, the main reason we should pray is to stay connected to the God we have entrusted with our lives and with the lives of our loved ones.

Unanswered Prayers

Ye lust, and have not: ye kill, and desire to have, and cannot obtain:
ye fight and war, yet ye have not, because ye ask not.
Ye ask, and receive not, because ye ask amiss,
that ye may consume it upon your lusts.
Ye adulterers and adulteresses,
know ye not that the friendship of the world is enmity with God? whosoever therefore
will be a friend of the world is the enemy of God.
(James 4:2-4 KJV)

Unanswered prayer is something that many Christians struggle with. Some have struggled with it so much that they have turned their backs on Christianity altogether. Others question God about it repeatedly, while there are those who believe that God does not answer prayer because there *is no* God. However, the reason for unanswered prayers is much simpler than we realize.

Sometimes our prayers go unanswered because we ask **amiss**.

Amiss – Not being in accordance with right order.
Not quite right; inappropriate or out of place.
Wrongly or inappropriately.

With those definitions in mind, we know that to ask amiss is to ask for the wrong reason. According to Strong's Exhaustive Concordance of the Bible, one of the words used to define amiss is evil, thus not only is the reason wrong, but it is evil. And anything wrong or evil is outside of God's will. Since it is not in our hearts to go to God for something with evil intentions, the question we should be asking is:

What is the right reason to ask God for something, for anything?

And this is the confidence that we have in him,
that, if we ask any thing according to his will, he heareth us:
And if we know that he hear us, whatsoever we ask, we know that we have the
petitions that we desired of him.
(1ˢᵗ John 5:14-15 KJV)

To determine if what you are asking God for is in His will, ask yourself this question: How does what you're praying for add to the church, advance the kingdom, or glorify God? If you cannot answer any of those questions, or if what you're asking for is not for any of those reasons, you may be asking amiss.

You see, as Christians we are here to do what God wills us to do, so much of the things we pray for should be those things that assist us in doing what is needed for the church, those things that get God the glory, and those things that advance the kingdom.

For example, many women ask God for a husband or many men ask God for a wife. But why? What is your purpose for wanting a spouse? Does it have something to do with the Kingdom? Does your desire somehow glorify God? If so, then according to scripture, your prayers will not only be heard, but granted. However, if your reason for asking is simply to satisfy yourself and your flesh, you run the risk of God not answering or not granting that prayer. Why? Because your reasons are self-*ish* and a marriage filled with self-*ish*ness can and oftentimes does lead to divorce.

And how does divorce reflect upon Christianity?

Not very good at all.

I am sure that some who read this are going to ask what having a spouse has to do with glorifying God, with adding to the church, or with adding to the kingdom. However, if that question has to be asked, that in and of itself says that the person asking *might not* be ready for the spouse for which they're asking.

Another thing that people are often praying for is money. However, why are they praying for money? Is at least some of it going to be used for a Godly purpose or is all of it going to be used for self-*ish* reasons? If there is no Godly reason or purpose motivating the prayer for money, God *may not* answer the prayer because the person praying *may be* asking amiss.

Now, does that mean that every prayer that is prayed amiss goes unanswered? No. However, it does mean that what you are praying for has nothing to do with love or with the Christian walk you have decided to take. It means what you have prayed for has no Godly purpose. And if God answers those ungodly prayers, you may have to endure the ungodly consequences of those ungodly prayers you have been granted.

Remember the saying, "Be careful what you ask for because you just might get it!"

Does any of that mean we should never pray for marriage or money? No. It means that you should know the Godly aspects of marriage and ask for those reasons *first*, all other reasons should be secondary. It means that you should be asking for money for Godly reasons *first* and all other reasons should be secondary. In fact, you should be asking for all things and looking for all things for a Godly reason *first* and every other reason should be secondary.

Why?

Because, as Christians, our goal is to fulfil God's vision. Thus, those things we ask for should be able to assist us in fulfilling His vision.

Should we never ask for anything for ourselves?

I'm not saying that.

What I am saying is:

But seek ye first the kingdom of God, and his righteousness; and all these things shall be added unto you.
(Matthew 6:33 KJV)

CHAPTER EIGHT

Christianity Requires Study

Study to shew thyself approved unto God, a workman that needeth not to be ashamed,
rightly dividing the word of truth.
(2 Timothy 2:15 KJV)

One of the main requirements of successful Christianity is study. Yet, many of us do not study. In fact, many of us do not even know what study is or how to study.

There are those of us who mistakenly believe that reading the Bible is the same as studying it. On the contrary, however, reading and studying the Bible are two completely different things. Then there are those of us who feel that going to weekly church Bible study is studying the Bible and some even feel that church Bible study is enough. However, attending Bible study only means that the pastor or the person teaching the bible study has studied and they are teaching you what they learned as a result of their studies.

Just as teachers in school and professors in college teach you what they have studied and it is up to you to go home and study what you have learned, the same applies to studying God's word. At Bible study you are taught, on your personal time you should study what you have been taught.

With this being said, the question that should follow is obvious and to answer that question, I'm going to use my own *very basic* study method as a demonstration.

What Is Study?

Well, according to Strong's Exhaustive Concordance of the Bible, a study book which gives us words in the original language in which the Bible is written, (in this case, archaic Greek) the word study, as it is used in 2nd Timothy 2:15 means – to make **effort**, to be **prompt** or **earnest**, to do diligence or be **diligent**, to **endeavor**, to **labor**, to **study**.

With this biblical breakdown of the word *study* in mind, and since the original Greek word, *study*, is defined by all of those words, it is here that you can and should take your study a step further by using a dictionary to look up the definition of each of these underlined words. Not only will this give you a deeper understanding of the word *study*, it will also give you a greater understanding of what it means to study according to 2nd Timothy 2:15.

Effort – Active or applied energy or force.

Prompt – To perform readily or immediately.

Earnest – Grave, Important. A serious and intent mental state.

Diligent – Steady, earnest or energetic effort.

Endeavor – Try or Attempt. To seriously or continually try, attempt to, or strive to do something.

Labor – Expenditure of physical and or mental effort.

Study – The activity or process of learning something by reading, memorizing facts, attending school, etc.
A state of contemplation.
Application of the mental faculties to the acquisition of knowledge.

After having defined each of these words, it is clear that to study the word of God according to 2nd Timothy is to seriously, actively, readily and continually apply your physical and mental energy and efforts to the mental acquisition of biblical knowledge and intelligence. To break it down even further, to study according to this particular scripture means to frequently and with serious intent focus on the word of God with the intention of gaining biblical intelligence.

Now that we know what the word study means in this scripture, we can also see the importance that God puts on us studying the Bible. If God wants studying His word to be that serious for us, we must trust Him enough to know that there is an equally, if not greater, reason why. Therefore, studying must be just as serious to us as it is to God. It should not be something one would take for granted or something that only half-hearted effort is put into.

If we are to study continually as 2nd Timothy says we should, that means that we will be on a never ending quest to learn all we can from the Bible. It means that we will repeat the Bible study process frequently and regularly, not whenever the whim hits us or whenever we have time. For this, it means that we should deem studying serious enough to *make* time.

Finally, to study the word of God according to 2nd Timothy means that we are and should always be putting forth energetic effort to learn the word and will of God, and that we are, and should always be committed to doing so.

What Should We Study?

Now that we know what studying is, the next question is what should we study?

The answer to that is simple.

What you should study first and foremost is the Bible. The Bible is the divinely inspired Word of God and for us to be successful at Christianity, to be successful at being reconciled to God, we need to know as much about Him as we can. Therefore, studying the Bible is of the utmost importance.

In addition to studying the Word of God, we should also study sermons. Whenever our pastors are preaching, we should not only be attentive, but we should remember the sermons, taking notes if need be. Then when we get into our personal Bible study time, we should study these sermons as we would study anything else dealing with the word of God.

The next thing on our study list should be whatever we learn at Bible study. Those topics should not just be studied within the walls of the church, but should also be studied within the walls of our homes and within the walls of our hearts. What we learn at church we should study at home, not only learning it for ourselves, but also learning it and applying it to our lives for those God has called us to love.

We should study those things we may be struggling with. For example, if anger is something we battle daily, studying anger in the Bible, seeing how it worked, seeing the negative effects of it, would help us to not only understand it, but to conquer it as well. It would teach us exactly what anger is and how it affects our Christian walk. And it would teach us that if anger is to be used, when, where, how, and why to effectively use it.

Because we are Christians that are called to love, studying love in the Bible would help us to properly exhibit that love in our daily lives and in our daily walk with God. Studying love would help us learn how and why to love and most importantly, studying love would help us to draw as many to Christ as is possible so that they could receive that love that saves the unsaved, heals the sick, and raises the dead.

There is a never ending list of things we can study in the Bible. There is also a never ending list of things about the bible we can study using methods that accompany the Bible. If we are ever unsure of what to study, we can always pray and ask God to give us the lesson or lessons He needs us to learn and study the most. We can also ask Him to give us the method or methods in which He needs us to learn or study it or them.

How Should We Study?

The first thing you have to do to study is commit to doing it and then exercise the discipline to stick to that commitment. Commitment can be hard at times, but not impossible. Just as you set aside to time to watch your favorite Tv show for a half hour or an hour, or listen to music, or visit your favorite social media website, that's the way you have to set aside time to study God's word.

Set a time each and every day for the purpose of study, a specific time, and stick to it no matter what. Get away from all people, unless it's a group study. Turn off all televisions, turn off all music players, turn off all phones, all tablets, all gaming systems, all computers, and dedicate that time to studying the word of God. It is much easier to study something when you are not surrounded by or bombarded with distractions.

Once you have set aside that time and have rid yourself of all distractions, find a space, preferably a private, quiet space, and gather your study tools. For a *basic study*, you'll need a few things. Number one, you'll need the Bible. Next, you'll need Strong's Exhaustive Concordance.

Strong's is a book filled with a complete alphabetical list of all the words written in the Bible. However, not only is every word in the Bible listed in Strong's, those words are accompanied by both a Hebrew and Greek Dictionary because the Bible was originally written in Hebrew (Old Testament) and Greek (New Testament). The Hebrew and Greek dictionaries are used to define those words as they were used in the original Hebrew and Greek languages, which gives us a better understanding of the meaning of each scripture. Lastly, unless you have a photographic memory, you'll need paper and whatever writing tools you deem necessary.

Once you have everything you need, pray.

Pray first!

Going into God's word without asking His assistance could lead to a very difficult and intimidating study in which you end that study knowing nothing more than you knew when you went into it. Thus, before you seek to understand God's word, ask God to help you with that understanding.

When you pray there are a few things you may consider asking God for to aid you in your studies. You can ask God to open your eyes so that you may clearly see His word in both the spirit and in the flesh. Ask God to open your ears so that you may hear His word. Ask God to open your heart so that you may receive His word whether you agree with it or not. Ask God to open your mind so that you may understand His word both naturally and supernaturally. And finally, ask God to expand your will so that you desire to live His word in times as tough as these.

The next thing you should do is select the subject of your study, be it a scripture where you study only one scripture for a deeper understanding or a topic where you study every instance of one particular word in the Bible to learn as much about that topic as you can.

If you are ever unsure of where to find topics, know that you are surrounded by them. You can choose Bible study topics you were taught at church, the topic of a sermon that was preached, or something that comes to your mind or heart. However, if none of those topics come to mind, pray and ask God to give you a topic. He will always lead you where He wants you to go. Once you have all that you need, open your books, open your mind, open your heart, and begin.

One method you can use is the one on the previous pages that explained the word *study*. However, instead of doing just a scriptural study where you only look at one scripture to understand it on a deeper level as we did a little bit with 2nd Timothy 2:15, you can do a topic study. A topic study is where you study every scripture using a certain word or topic to get a better understanding of that word or topic.

For example, you can do an Old Testament study using only Old Testament scriptures that contain a certain word or that contain your topic of choice. You can do a New Testament study using only New Testament scriptures that contain that word or that topic. Or you can study every scripture in the entire Bible that contains that particular word or that particular topic.

To give a demonstration of a topic study, we are going to look up all scriptures in the New Testament about a certain topic. Once again, we're going to study the word *study*.

Throughout the entire bible, the word study is used only three times, once in the Old Testament and twice in the New Testament. I demonstrated the word *study* in the New Testament by using the scripture in 2nd Timothy. In this example we are going to add the other instance in the New Testament where the word study was used, taking the study from scriptural to topic.

*And that ye **study** to be quiet, and to do your own business, and to work with your own hands, as we commanded you;*
(1st Thessalonians 4:11 KJV)

According to Strong's Exhaustive Concordance, the word study in this particular scripture is given the number 5389. Because this is a New Testament scripture, we know that the New Testament was written in Greek. With that being said, we turn to the Greek dictionary in the back of the book and search for the number 5389.

Once we find that number, we are given the following definition:

Emulous – (**_eager_** or **_earnest_** to do something) **_labor, strive, study._**

For every word that Strong's gives as a description of the Greek definition, we deepen our study by looking those words up in another dictionary to gain a complete understanding of what we are studying.

<u>**Emulous**</u> – Seeking to emulate or imitate someone or something.

<u>**Eager**</u> – Urgent or enthusiastic desire or intent.

<u>**Earnest**</u> – An intensely serious state of mind.
        Serious intent and Sober.
        Grave or Important.

<u>**Labor**</u> – Physical or mental effort.
        To work.
        To move with great effort.

<u>**Strive**</u> – To make effort.
        To labor hard.

<u>**Study**</u> – The use of the mind to gain knowledge.
        To consider attentively or in detail.

Based on Strong's definition of the Greek word *study* and based on the definitions of the other words Strong's gave as further description, we should gather that in 1st Thessalonians 4:11 (KJV), the word study means that we should seriously and enthusiastically seek and put great effort into being silent, minding and doing our own business, and working with our hands.

If we are to really meditate on that scripture, we would see that if we do what 2nd Thessalonians says we should do, it could keep us out of a lot of unnecessary trouble. It would also help us to walk honestly and to have a lack of nothing according to 1st Thessalonians 4:12 (KJV). Thus, studying gives you understanding that just reading oftentimes cannot.

Why Should We Study?

The first reason we should study is so that we can learn all about God whom we serve and whom we are called to be reconciled to. We should study the Bible to learn about Jesus, the One who saves us, the One who died so that we can live. And we should study the Bible to learn about The Holy Spirt, the One who guides us all into all truth and the One that makes intercession for us.

The next reason we should study the Bible is so that we can know how to love. Christianity is a call to love and therefore we should study the book that teaches us how to love, the book that teaches us how to call others to love, and the book that teaches us how to walk out this love the way God has called us to.

Without study we will struggle in our walk.

With study we will be strengthened in our walk.

And finally, we should study to shew ourselves approved unto God, a workman that needeth not to be ashamed, rightly dividing the word of truth.

CHAPTER NINE

Christianity Requires Commitment

Jesus said unto him, Thou shalt love the Lord thy God with all thy heart, and with all thy soul, and with all thy mind.
(Matthew 22:37 KJV)

Commitment.

Anything you have ever really wanted in your life and have actually attained was because of commitment. You dreamed about what you wanted, planned for that dream, set goals for it, and took each and every step needed to complete those goals. When everything was done, when all ducks were in a row and all work was complete, you had what you really wanted. Because you committed to getting it.

Christianity, to walk it out successfully, requires that same level of commitment.

What Is Commitment?

Commitment, by definition, is the state or quality of being dedicated to a cause, activity, etc. It is the determination or the will to do a certain thing, live a certain way, be a certain type of person. In Christianity, commitment is the dedication to God and the determination to obey His commandments by living as, doing what, and believing what Christ did.

One of the things that will help you in your commitment to Christianity is remembering that Christianity does not center on you. You are committed to God and to His purpose, not to you and to your purpose. It is not about you getting God to do whatever you want Him to do for you, it's about you doing whatever God calls you to do for the church.

Just as Jesus did.

Christianity is grave business that requires a lot. It is not something you do in your spare time or whenever you get a chance. It is not something you do for show, not something you are in name only. It comes with great responsibility and necessitates much.

Christianity requires commitment.

To shed a different light on commitment, let's view it from a different perspective. Let's say that commitment to Christianity is like commitment to marriage. Just as husband and wife have vowed their fidelity to one another, in Christianity, Christians vow their fidelity to God through Jesus Christ. Christ is the husband, the head in this Christian union, and Christians are His spouse.

In marriage, just as the wife becomes a part of the husband's family and the husband gives the wife his last name so that she is identified as belonging to him and to his family, in Christianity, Christ gives you the name Christ-*ian* so that you are identified as His or as belonging to His family. He also gives you the authority to use His name while you are walking out your Christianity here on earth.

In a marriage there are vows. In Christianity there are vows.

What is a vow?

> **Vow** - A serious or solemn promise to do something or some things and to behave in a certain way.

In traditional Christian marriage vows, the husband and wife vow things to one another. The husband vows to take the bride as his wedded wife, to have and to hold her from the day of their marriage and going forward, for better and for worse, for richer and for poorer, in sickness and in health, to love, honor, and cherish her until death parts them.

In traditional Christian marriage, the bride vows to take the groom as her wedded husband, to have and to hold him from the day of their marriage and going forward, for better and for worse, for richer and for poorer, in sickness and in health, to love, honor, cherish, and *obey* him until death parts them.

In Christianity, because of and through God's son, Jesus, we make vows to God and God makes vows to us. We vow to believe in God's son, to obey God's commandments, to love God's people and to love God with everything in us. In return, God vows to take us as His own, as part of his family, but that's not all. As a member of God's family there are other vows he makes to us as well.

God vows to love you.

> *For God so loved the world, that he gave his only begotten Son, that whosoever believeth in him should not perish, but have everlasting life.*
> *(John 3:16 KJV)*

God vows to spare your soul from eternal damnation.

> *That if thou shalt confess with thy mouth the Lord Jesus, and shalt believe in thine heart that God hath raised him from the dead, thou shalt be saved.*
> *(Romans 10:9 KJV)*

God vows to provide for you.

> *But my God shall supply all your need according to his riches in glory by Christ Jesus.*
> *(Philippians 4:19 KJV)*

He vows to keep you safe and protected.

> *The Lord shall preserve thee from all evil: he shall preserve thy soul.*
> *The Lord shall preserve thy going out and thy coming in from this time forth, and even for evermore.*
> *(Psalm 121:7-8 KJV)*

God vows to bear your burdens.

Come unto me, all ye that labour and are heavy laden, and I will give you rest.
Take my yoke upon you, and learn of me; for I am meek and lowly in heart: and ye shall
find rest unto your souls.
For my yoke is easy, and my burden is light.
(Matthew 11:28-30 KJV)

God vows to comfort you.

Blessed be God, even the Father of our Lord Jesus Christ,
the Father of mercies, and the God of all comfort;
Who comforteth us in all our tribulation,
that we may be able to comfort them which are in any trouble,
by the comfort wherewith we ourselves are comforted of God.
(2nd Corinthians 1:3-4 KJV)

And finally, God vows to bless you.

Blessed are the poor in spirit: for theirs is the kingdom of heaven.
Blessed are they that mourn: for they shall be comforted.
Blessed are the meek: for they shall inherit the earth.
Blessed are they which do hunger and thirst after righteousness: for they shall be filled.
Blessed are the merciful: for they shall obtain mercy.
Blessed are the pure in heart: for they shall see God.
Blessed are the peacemakers: for they shall be called the children of God.
Blessed are they which are persecuted for righteousness' sake: for theirs is the kingdom of
heaven.
Blessed are ye, when men shall revile you, and persecute you, and shall say all manner of
evil against you falsely, for my sake.
Rejoice, and be exceeding glad: for great is your reward in heaven: for so persecuted
they the prophets which were before you.
(Matthew 5:3-12)

As we can see, our relationship with Christ is one that is reciprocal. In exchange for the life we live for Christ, God vows to take care of us. No, not in the financial sense, although that *is* a part of it, but God vows to take care of *every* need we have.

If we look at *healthy* relationships, we can clearly see that when two people come together, they commit or dedicate themselves to having one particular person as their significant other. It is in this dedication to another that a person will do what it takes to make their spouse happy. As Christians, we have entered into a loving relationship with God and we should be committed to that loving relationship and to the success of it.

Just as committed as God is.

What We Commit To.

We commit to God and His word.

No servant can serve two masters:
for either he will hate the one, and love the other;
or else he will hold to the one, and despise the other. Ye cannot serve God and
mammon.
(Luke 16:13 KJV)

It is at this point you should know that, as a Christian, not only are you committing to a life of Godly purpose, you are committing to a life of service. You are committing to a life of study, a life of witnessing, a life of obedience. You are committing to a life of faith, and most importantly you are committing to a life of love.

You are committing to Kingdom business.

Because *you* are Kingdom business.

As such, you can't make the Kingdom be about your agenda, you have to be about the Kingdom's agenda. Because if you're about *your* business and God is about *your* business, who's about Kingdom business? Who's about God's business?

No one.

That's why this Christian relationship is a reciprocal thing. Whatever God calls you to do, that's your service to the kingdom, your part in the construction of the church. Again, your very life is your ministry. Thus, your life should reflect God and the Kingdom of God. And for that, God will supply all of your needs.

How Do We Commit?

How do we commit to God?
The first act of commitment is to have no other God's before Him.

> *Thou shalt have no other gods before me.*
> *(Exodus 20:3 KJV)*

How do we have no other God's before Him?
You do not put anything before God.
Not your spouse. Not your parents. Not your children. Not your job. Not your wants and desires. Not material possessions. Nothing.

> *If any man come to me, and hate not his father, and mother,*
> *and wife, and children, and brethren, and sisters,*
> *yea, and his own life also, he cannot be my disciple.*
> *(Luke 14:26 KJV)*

Now many people have read this scripture and struggled with it, often wondering how God could require such a commitment that he would ask you to hate everyone and to hate your own life just to follow Him. However, it is at this juncture that the word hate needs to be explained so that we can have a greater understanding of the level of commitment God requires.

The word hate here comes from the Greek word Miseo. Miseo comes from the primary Greek word, Misos. Misos means to hate, as in detest to the point of persecution. That is how those who crucified Christ felt about Him, but that is not how He's asking us to feel about those we love.

The word Miseo, a derivative of the word Misos, means to hate in the sense that you love a person less. Less than what? Less than you love Christ, less than you love God. It means that there should never be *anyone* or any*thing* that comes before God. Because there is no way God would tell you to love His people and then turn around in the next breath and tell you to hate them. Thus, the word hate here does not mean hate in the sense that we know it, the word hate here means to love less than you love God.

That is the level of commitment God requires from us.

Him first, everything else after.

At this point, many of you may be wondering how things and people can be put before God. It's actually very simple.

There are some that have desires for things, material things, or people and their desires are so strong that they are willing to get what they want by any means necessary.

Let's take it even farther and use a husband as an example.

Let's say there is a woman that wants a husband and has wanted one from the time she was a child. Every thought the woman has is about getting a husband. She looks at every man as if he could be her husband. She dresses to attain a husband. She learns to do things that would please a husband. Her every thought is about getting and having a husband. Her every action is geared toward getting a husband.

Here is the problem with this scenario:

The woman is putting her desire for a husband before her desire for God. You see, she can't have her *every* thought be on attaining a husband, because if her *every* thought is on a husband, then *none* of her thoughts are on God. If her *every* thought is on pleasing a husband, then *none* of her thoughts are on pleasing God. If her *every* action is geared toward getting a husband, then *none* of her actions are geared toward God. Thus, she loves the thought of getting a husband more than she loves the idea of living for God.

She has made getting a husband her god.

And if God ever did bless her with a husband, based on her actions and thoughts before she got that husband, what do you think she would do with him? She would make that husband her god and give him a higher priority in her life than she gives God.

That's not the way God wants it to be.

God wants it to be Him first and everything else after.

God's will first and every other thing we will should be secondary.

Because life can oftentimes be very hard, you will be faced with moments, many moments, when you have to choose between what God wills, what you will, and what someone else wills. You will have to choose between what God wants, what you want, and what someone else wants. As Christians, we should always choose what we know God wills, what we know God wants us to choose, but many of us won't do that.

If we don't have the level of commitment God requires us to have, the flesh will get in the way of the choices we make. The heart will get in the way. Emotions will get in the way. Even our own minds will betray us and get in the way. As much as we would like to always choose God, many times we won't. However, to continue on with our commitment, we have to put Him and His will before anything we want, will, or desire. Because He should be first.

Our dedication should be to Him first.
Our service should be to Him first.
Our obedience should be to Him first.
Our trust should be in Him first.
Our love should be for Him first.
Our souls should belong to Him only.
That is commitment, the kind of commitment we should give to God.

Why Should We Commit?

We should commit to God because God is infinite in His wisdom.

O the depth of the riches both of the wisdom and knowledge of God! how unsearchable are his judgments, and his ways past finding out!
(Romans 11:33 KJV)

He is without flaw.

As for God, his way is perfect: the word of the Lord is tried: he is a buckler to all those that trust in him.
(Psalm 18:30 KJV)

He is forgiving.

If we confess our sins, he is faithful and just to forgive us our sins and to cleanse us from all unrighteousness.
(1 John 1:9 KJV)

He is merciful.

For thou, Lord, art good, and ready to forgive; and plenteous in mercy unto all them that call upon thee.
(Psalm 86:5 KJV)

He is powerful.

Great is our Lord, and of great power: his understanding is infinite.
(Psalm 147:5 KJV)

He is all seeing and all knowing.

> *Thou knowest my downsitting and mine uprising,*
> *thou understandest my thought afar off.*
> *Thou compassest my path and my lying down,*
> *and art acquainted with all my ways.*
> *(Psalm 139:2-3 KJV)*

God will never lie to you.

> *God is not a man, that he should lie;*
> *neither the son of man, that he should repent: hath he said, and shall he not do it?*
> *or hath he spoken, and shall he not make it good?*
> *(Numbers 23:19 KJV)*

God will never leave you.

> *Let your conversation be without covetousness;*
> *and be content with such things as ye have: for he hath said,*
> *I will never leave thee, nor forsake thee.*
> *(Hebrews 13:5 KJV)*

God loves you more than anyone else.

> *Greater love hath no man than this,*
> *that a man lay down his life for his friends.*
> *(John 15:13 KJV)*

And at the end of the day God wants to bless you more than anyone else.

> *Blessed is the man that trusteth in the Lord,*
> *and whose hope the Lord is.*
> *(Jeremiah 17:7 KJV)*

And

For I know the thoughts that I think toward you, saith the Lord, thoughts of peace,
and not of evil, to give you an expected end.
(Jeremiah 29:11 KJV)

Now, knowing all of this about God, out of everyone you have ever met in your entire life, can you say that you have ever met a person like that?

For all of us that answer would be no.

There is no one like God, not one.

It is for *that* reason that we should commit to God. Especially since He will and does, without flaw and without wavering, always commit to us.

CHAPTER TEN

Christianity Requires Surrender

Then said Jesus unto his disciples,
If any man will come after me,
let him deny himself, and take up his cross, and follow me.
For whosoever will save his life shall lose it:
and whosoever will lose his life for my sake shall find it.
(Matthew 16:24-25 KJV)

As we established from the very beginning, Christianity is all about love. It is about loving God and loving God's people to the point where you will do anything God requires of you to ensure the salvation of their souls. You will do these things whether you understand what God requires of you or whether you agree with what God requires of you or not. Your main goal, care, and concern is that none should perish, that none should be eternally separated from God. The same way God cared and cares for you, that is the same way you should care for others.

Enter surrender.

To surrender to God means that you should leave no part of your life unavailable to Him. It means that you will not fight Him in any area of your life. It means you give all of you to God for His use, for His will, and for His purpose. You surrender all.

<u>Surrender</u> – To yield to the power, control, or possession of another upon compulsion or demand.
To give up completely or agree to forgo especially in favor of another.
To give oneself up into the power of another.
To give oneself over to something.

Now as we have established, Christianity requires you to surrender things to God, many things. However, we're only going to discuss four of those things. Four things that will make your walk with Christ much easier.

Obedience, the surrender of your actions.

Sacrifice, the surrender of your will.

Tithes, the surrender of your money.

Forgiveness, the surrender of your emotions.

A Relationship with God Requires Obedience.

But be ye doers of the word, and not hearers only, deceiving your own selves.
For if any be a hearer of the word, and not a doer,
he is like unto a man beholding his natural face in a glass:
For he beholdeth himself, and goeth his way,
and straightway forgetteth what manner of man he was.
But whoso looketh into the perfect law of liberty, and continueth therein,
he being not a forgetful hearer, but a doer of the work,
this man shall be blessed in his deed.
(James 1:22-25 KJV)

Christianity requires obedience.

It requires you to do what God commands you to do when He commands it, the way in which He commands you to do it. It does not necessarily mean you will understand or even agree with what is commanded of you, but you are required to obey the commandments, nevertheless. Because we know and are guaranteed that whatever God requires us to do, it is out of love for Him and for His people.

We know that God will never require us to break the law, not man's law and definitely not His law. We know that what is required of us is required to bring us or someone else closer to Him. And we know that what is required of us is for the building of the church by the saving of lost souls.

With that being said, the question we should all be asking is:

What is Obey?

Obey – To do what someone tells you to do or what a rule, law, etc., says you must do.
To follow the commands or guidance of.
To conform to or comply with.

In Christianity, obedience is a surrender of your actions to God for a Godly purpose.

What Should We Obey?

Whatever God tells us to obey.
Scripture says we should be hearers and doers of the word. Thus, whatever the word says we should do and whatever God says we should do, that is what we should do.

When Should We Obey?

Whenever God tells us to obey.
Delaying obedience can only delay blessings, delay deliverance, delay healing. Delaying obedience will never be good to you or to anyone that is dependent upon your obedience. For instance, in the Bible, when Jonah delayed obeying what God told him to do, many people were affected negatively by that delay.

God told Jonah to head to Nineveh and cry against it, telling the people there to repent and turn from their wicked ways. Because Jonah did not want God to have mercy on Nineveh, he chose to get on a boat that was going to Tarshish and not to Nineveh.

While Jonah was on that boat, because of his delay in obedience, a great wind came upon the sea and the mariners on that boat suffered terror. In addition, those people, not knowing about Jonah's disobedience, suffered loss. They were so consumed with saving their lives and stopping the boat from being torn apart by the storm that they decided to throw their belongings and whatever else was on the boat overboard, trying to lighten the boat.

What did they lose when they threw things overboard? Were the things thrown overboard of great value to the people? No one knows, but whatever it was, greatly valued or not, it was lost to them and their lives when they felt the need to save their lives. All because Jonah chose to do what he wanted and not what God wanted him to do.

In addition, when the others on the boat finally learned that Jonah was the problem, he asked them to toss him overboard instead of jumping overboard himself, adding mental torment to the loss the mariners already incurred. Why mental torment? Because for the rest of their lives they were going to remember and endure the thought that they had to toss a living man into a raging sea where he would more than likely be killed to save themselves.

How did that, knowing they may have killed a man, affect them? And for how long?

However, it does not end there, after being tossed into the sea, Jonah was swallowed by a great fish and lived in the belly of that fish for three days and three nights. All because of his disobedience. So not only did his delay in obedience negatively affect him, it negatively affected all he came into contact with. But had he done what God commanded him to do when God commanded him to do it, he would have spared not only himself the undue suffering that he experienced, but he would have spared the others their suffering as well.

It is for that reason that we should obey God and obey Him immediately.

Why should we obey?

We should obey because as Christians we have joined in covenant with God to live as Christ did and the main thing Christ did was obey God. We should obey because as Christians we have agreed to love God's people and obeying God is an act of that love, both for God and for God's people.

We should obey because we trust God. We might not always know why God has asked us to do or say something, but we know that His word says all things work together for good for them that love God and are the called according to His purpose (Romans 8:28). Thus, we know that in our obedience we are doing good. And finally, we should obey because if God called us to do anything, that calling shows that He finds us trustworthy and capable. It shows that He trusts us to do what He assigned us to do. It shows that not only do we have faith in Him, but that He also has faith in us.

A Relationship With God Requires Sacrifice.

I beseech you therefore, brethren, by the mercies of God,
that ye present your bodies a living sacrifice, holy, acceptable unto God,
which is your reasonable service.
(Romans 12:1 KJV)

Sacrifice.

When you volunteer your life to Christ, that act is a commitment to surrender your will to God and to sacrifice your life just as Christ did. The difference, however, is that the sacrifice of your life and the surrender of your will is acted out with every day you live. Jesus' sacrifice was acted out with His life *and* with a crucifixion.

Although you may not be dying on a cross for all to see, you are dying nevertheless. You are volunteering to die daily to and of this world so that you and others may live eternally for and in the world that is to come. And you are doing it for all the world to see.

You are dying to this world by the surrender of your will to fleshly and worldly things. For example, surrendering your will is so that you won't be so focused on the world and what you want that you ignore what God is calling you to do. Sacrificing your will is so that you don't begin to feel or believe that what God is calling you to do is getting in the way of what you want to do and thus start to sacrifice God's will instead.

Now, does that mean you should never will or desire anything?

No.

It means that you should never will or desire anything more than you will and desire God and His will and His vision for mankind. It means that in choosing to live for God as Christ did, you are acknowledging that your life is not your own. Your life, the life God has blessed you with, belongs to Him and thus should be lived for Him, for the purpose He has called you to live.

That purpose is the great commission.

The saving of souls by leading mankind to Christ who can and will reconcile them to God.

Once you understand that your life is not your own, you can better walk out your Christianity. And in walking out that love you will clearly see that love, that great, altruistic, Godly love comes with great sacrifice.

It comes with surrendering your will.

What Is Sacrifice?

<u>Sacrifice</u> – An act of slaughtering an animal or person or surrendering a possession as an offering to God or to a divine supernatural figure.

The act of giving up something that you want to keep, especially in order to get or do something or to help someone.

In Christianity, the sacrifice is you. You are, in a sense, slaughtering your flesh, giving up what you want, and presenting yourself as an offering to God to help others.

What We Should Sacrifice.

We should sacrifice our lives.

Just as Christ did.

Sacrifice, to us, feels like one of the most unnatural acts in existence. It means that we can't give our minds and bodies what *we feel* they need or want. Instead, we must give our minds and bodies what *God knows* they need and want, and it means we are doing it for God and for others.

However, the difficulty in sacrifice comes from not knowing why we are sacrificing. It comes from not knowing that in Christianity our lives are not our own. Our lives belong to God just as Jesus' life did. We must understand that we are Christians, that means we are followers of Christ. Christ lived here on earth doing not what He willed, but doing what God willed. That is what we should be doing, living for God and not for self.

We should understand that Christ's sacrifice was not just limited to the cross, His sacrifice was exhibited in every day He lived, in everything He did, and in every word that came out of His mouth. He sacrificed everything. And He did it for God and for us. As Christians, that is what we are here to do.

Sacrifice for God and for others.

To sacrifice self in this manner requires strength and understanding. We must understand why we are sacrificing ourselves, for what purpose the sacrifice is. Also, we must ask God for the strength to sacrifice self in favor of someone or in favor of something greater than we are. Especially when that sacrifice may feel unwarranted or unappreciated by those we are sacrificing for. However, we must remember that God sees and appreciates the sacrifice even if man does not.

To further explain, we must also understand that sacrifice does not require agreement, meaning that we do not have to agree with what we are sacrificing or even why we are sacrificing. We must simply trust God and know that if He or His word says something should be said or done, as the creator, He has deeper insight into His creation and knows what's best. Therefore, if God or God's word says to do it or not do it, to say it or not say it, to deny it or not deny it, we should sacrifice our will in favor of His.

To go against God and do what we want instead of what He wants says several things. First it says that we think we know better than God does. Next, it says that we don't care about the Kingdom or about what God wants. It says that we are ignorant, sometimes willfully, of and to the God we have claimed to serve. It says that our needs or desires are more important than the needs, will, and desires of God. And it says that we have chosen to, willfully or ignorantly, deny the Spirit of God.

However, we must know that to deny the Spirit is to give in to the flesh. It is to give in to what we want and to oppose what God wants. So how can we truly walk in love, how can we truly walk as Christians if we're walking in the flesh, if we're walking against God? The truth of the matter is that we can't.

We live in a society where everyone is looking out for themselves. As a result of that, some feel as though they have to look out for themselves as well because they know that no one else is looking out for them. That is a form of self-preservation. However, in Christianity, it is not about preserving self, it is about preserving the church.

That is the reason for sacrifice.

Even if no one is looking out for you, you should still be looking out for them. Because at the end of it all, man may be preserving self, but God, because of your sacrifice, is preserving you.

Why Should We Sacrifice.

We should sacrifice because we do not want to be a hindrance or a stumbling block to another person. We should sacrifice because we do not want to be a hindrance or a stumbling block to the church. We should sacrifice because we want to do God's will and not to go against His will. And we should sacrifice because He has trusted us enough to assign us whatever sacrifice He requires of us.

Just as He trusted Jesus.

Jesus, in the Garden of Gethsemane, exercised self-denial and sacrifice of the most excruciating kind. You see, Jesus wanted to *not* suffer the torture of the crucifixion. He knew what was to come, knew how great the suffering would be, and desired not to endure such cruelty. However, despite His desire to *not* suffer the agony of the cross and all things leading up to it, He, in absolute obedience to God, chose to deny himself the desire to *not* be subjected to the cross, and did what God sent Him to do. That was and is self-denial and self-sacrifice of the greatest and most unmatched kind.

In Christianity, the majority of things we are required to deny ourselves of are things that can harm another. There are times that we wish to do things we do not see as harmful, but that are actually detrimental to the church of God. For that reason, we have to lean not on our own understanding, but trust completely in God, knowing that what He requires of us is what is best for His church and for His vision.

Does sacrificing so much mean that we cannot have fun?

On the contrary, it means just the opposite.

You see, God does indeed want you to have fun, to have joy, to have pleasure. If that was not the case, He would not have placed Adam and Eve in the Garden of Eden.

What does the Garden of Eden have to do with pleasure?

A lot.

The word Eden means pleasure and delight.

Thus, He placed them in a garden of pleasure, a garden where they could experience all of the good God had to offer. Today, people want to experience all of the pleasure that the world has to offer and oftentimes that worldly pleasure separates us from God. Today, the world has convinced people that in Christianity there is no fun, no joy, no pleasure.

However, their false belief comes from the fact that they have allowed the world to tell them what is right and wrong. They have allowed the world to tell them what is good and what is not. They have allowed the world to separate them from God while at the same time condemning them for going toward God.

So how can a people who don't know God tell you that walking with God is not fun, or pleasurable, or delightful?

They can't.

They can only lead you to the pleasure they know, a pleasure that leads to death.

And it is for that reason that we should sacrifice our lives and live for God, sacrificing daily for the salvation of souls.

CHAPTER ELEVEN

Christianity Requires Surrender
(Part Two)

I am crucified with Christ: nevertheless I live; yet not I, but Christ liveth in me: and the life which I now live in the flesh I live by the faith of the Son of God, who loved me, and gave himself for me.
(Galatians 2:20 KJV)

Now that we have an understanding of the first two things we are to surrender to God in our Christianity, we can move forward to the remaining two.

Tithes and Forgiveness.

The two that seem to be the hardest.

A Relationship With God Requires Tithes

Will a man rob God? Yet ye have robbed me. But ye say, Wherein have we robbed thee? In tithes and offerings.
(Malachi 3:8 KJV)

Tithes.

A word in the Christian community that for some is cause for heated debate. For some outside of the Christian community, it's the source of ridicule.

Why are you giving your money to the church? I thought the word of God was supposed to be free.

Why are you giving your money to the pastor? He's driving around in new cars, living in a good house, dressing in the finest clothes, and eating good while the members of his church are dirt poor and struggling.

Why are you giving your money to the church? You can give it to someone in need, that way you know where it goes.

Why are you giving your money to the church? That's old testament doctrine, you don't have to do that anymore.

Why are you giving your money to the church? They're not doing right with it anyway.

And on and on and on.

However, what those asking the questions do not know or don't understand is that tithes are not about where the money goes.

Why?

Because even though tithes have been or may be used for wrong and ungodly purposes, it is also oftentimes used for good. Oftentimes it goes to pay for the church which may still be under mortgage. It goes to pay for electricity so that church members can have church comfortably. It goes to pay for water so that the church can be cleaned. Tithes pays for those things required to keep a building up and running in addition to helping those in need.

However, even deeper than the surface is that tithes are about obedience to God. It's about trusting God. It's about you performing God's will even when you think or know others are not or may not be. It's about you loving God more than the ten percent He's asking you to give.

Tithing is about faith.

Tithing is a demonstration to God that no matter what is going on around you, good or bad, no matter how honest or dishonest, no matter how honorable or dishonorable others may be or are being, you will still trust God, you will still have faith in His word and in His promises, and you will still remain faithful. Tithing is a demonstration that there is not a part of you that you will not surrender, your money included.

However, tithing is not just about how faithful you will be to God, it is also about how faithful God will be to you. In His word God said that there are promises that come with tithing.

Bring ye all the tithes into the storehouse, that there may be meat in mine house, and prove me now herewith, saith the Lord of hosts, if I will not open you the windows of heaven, and pour you out a blessing, that there shall not be room enough to receive it. And I will rebuke the devourer for your sakes, and he shall not destroy the fruits of your ground; neither shall your vine cast her fruit before the time in the field, saith the Lord of hosts. And all nations shall call you blessed: for ye shall be a delightsome land, saith the Lord of hosts.
(Malachi 3:10-12 KJV)

At the end of it all, tithing is a demonstration of your faithfulness to God. After all, you're in a relationship with Him and tithing just so happens to be a part of your relationship. The part that communicates to God that you will do what He commands you to do. And the part where God blesses you for doing what He commands you to do.

It's reciprocal.

Because you are in a relationship with God.

A *reciprocal relationship.*

A Relationship With God Requires Forgiveness.

For if ye forgive men their trespasses,
your heavenly Father will also forgive you:
But if ye forgive not men their trespasses,
neither will your Father forgive your trespasses.
(Matthew 6:14-15 KJV)

Forgiveness.

The source of much debate.

A topic many do not understand.

Forgiveness, for many, is a tough subject. Many don't know what it is and even more don't know how to do it. Some people view forgiveness as a demonstration of weakness, they view it as allowing people to hurt or harm them while doing nothing in return. This lack of vengeance, this perceived holding back of justice brings about feelings of resentment and bitterness, resentment toward the individual responsible for the hurt and offense and bitterness toward God for allowing it to happen and for not allowing us to fight back.

However, for a person to feel that way when it comes to forgiveness means that forgiveness is not really understood. Thus, the question we should be asking is:

What Is Forgiveness?

According to Strong's Concordance the definition of the word forgive is to send forth, to lay aside, to leave, to let alone, to let go, to let be, to let have, to **omit**, to put or send away, to **remit**, to **suffer**, to **yield up**.

Omit – To leave out someone or something.
> To not include someone or something.
> To fail to do something.

Remit – To lay aside a mood or disposition partly or wholly.
> To desist from an activity.
> To release from the guilt or penalty of.
> To refrain from exacting.
> To cancel or refrain from inflicting.
> To give relief from suffering.
> To restore or consign to a former status or condition.

Yield up – To give up and cease resistance or **contention**.

Contention – Anger or disagreement.

After looking at these definitions of the word forgive, we should now understand that forgiveness is releasing a person from a wrongdoing or an offense we hold them at fault for. It is releasing them from a debt that we feel they owe to us. It is us refraining from exacting revenge on a person as a result of that debt, that wrongdoing, or that offense. However, forgiveness is a much deeper than that.

Forgiveness is also understanding that even though a person may have done you wrong, they *may* have been used by the devil to hurt you and don't know it. If the devil is using them to hurt you, to hurt or abuse them further as a result of the wrong they've done to you only adds hurt to a person that the devil is already hurting.

A person may hurt you because they don't know God. To exact revenge on that person is to help them to continue not knowing God by your ungodly actions. However, to forgive them of their actions is to introduce them to the God they do not know, and that forgiveness starts the process of extracting them from the devil they do know. In order to do this though, you have to turn your emotions over to God.

Why?

Because forgiveness, in Christianity, is a surrender of your emotions to God.

And how do we turn our emotions over to God?

We focus on God and on doing God's will instead of focusing on the problem or on the person causing the problem. You see, forgiveness means you are allowing God's will to mean more to you than the other person's offense. It means you have cancelled the debt you feel the other person owes and that you are moving forward with God in doing His will. Forgiveness is an act of love that prevents you from being so emotionally and mentally distracted by people and by circumstances that you can't obey God's calling on you and on your life.

With unforgiveness, however, you can't focus on God enough to do what He called you to do because you're mad or hurt or feeling betrayed. All of the time you spend experiencing those negative emotions and those negative thoughts takes away from the time you could be spending with God, time you could be using to do God's will, time you could be spending directing a soul to Christ.

But not only that.

If we were to act out our vengeance, us and our vengeful actions could be the reason some or many remain separated from Christ. And that would be wrong, especially since the entirety of Christianity is about love and restoration, not about anger and separation.

And unforgiveness promotes separation from God.

How?

Unforgiveness leads to uncontrolled or unrestrained emotions like hate. Unrestrained emotions like hate leads to sin, sin like ungodly actions. Ungodly actions can lead to hate crimes and hate crimes could lead to murder.

And how does hate, murder, and ungodly actions reflect on Christians and on Christianity as a whole? How does hate, murder, and ungodly actions lead anyone to Christ? How does hate, ungodly actions and murder help the family you have now victimized as a result of your unforgiveness?

The truth of the matter is that it reflects on Christianity in such a negative manner that it can stop souls from being saved. It leads no one to Christ, but instead sends people running as far away from Christianity as they can get. And it destroys the friends and family of the victim, a victim who was still a child of God whether you liked what they were doing or saying or not. All unforgiveness does is takes a soul away before that person had a chance to know Christ, to love God. And it takes away the time a person had left to live, time that could have led to their soul being saved and to them leading others to have saved souls as well. It prevents said soul, if the soul was unsaved, from gaining salvation as God wills for us all and possibly from doing major things in the kingdom of God.

That is why we should be quick to forgive, quick to prevent the devil from gaining a foothold on us, on the church. When we are unable to forgive someone because of something we feel they did wrong, even something we feel they said or did against the kingdom or the church, hurting, harming, or even something as extreme as killing them does not change the offensive action. In reality, it hurts the church, it hurts the kingdom, it hurts Christianity. It hurts God's people, the same people He commanded us to love.

Why?

Because it demonstrates to them that we Christians are hateful, harmful, unloving and ungodly people.

It shows them that our emotions are uncontrolled and ungodly.

It shows them that our actions are uncontrolled and ungodly.

And it further separates them from the God they now believe we, the uncontrolled and judgmental, serve.

Why?

Because we sinned against them in reaction to their sin against us.

And how does their sin against us justify us turning around and sinning against them?

It does not!

Thus, forgiveness is not just for you or just for the other person, forgiveness is for everyone. It is for the saved and unsaved alike. It is for the people that God called us to love.

Moreover, the devil uses unforgiveness as a distraction to keep you from doing God's will. If you are so caught up in your emotions that it distracts you from doing what God has called you to do, the kingdom suffers. But if you can give your emotions over to God and remain focused on your calling no matter what, the kingdom wins.

All because you surrendered your emotions to God.

And if forgiveness is still hard for you even after reading this, ask yourself a question.

Why does it matter?

Why does the wrong someone did matter?

The truth is that it only matters to your pride.

And we all know that pride in Christianity is not often a good thing.

With that being said, look at offenses from another perspective. If someone does you wrong, don't allow yourself to think they did it intentionally. However, even if they did do it intentionally, why does it matter enough to anger you or upset you? Why does it matter enough to possibly make you do something that falsely reflects Christianity and give Christianity a bad name? Why does it matter enough to make you step outside of God's love?

It shouldn't.

You see, as Christians we love one another, we don't wish harm on each other. Thus, if we don't wish harm on them, if we don't wish God to harm them, if we know we aren't going to harm them, why does it matter if they did us or the kingdom or the church wrong?

The truth of the matter is that it shouldn't.

Why?

Because we love them, and love should be all that matters.

Besides…

Dearly beloved, avenge not yourselves, but rather give place unto wrath: for it is written, Vengeance is mine; I will repay, saith the Lord.
(Romans 12:19 KJV)

In Summation…

For Christianity to work and to be effective in your life and in the life of others, it requires surrender to God.

Complete and total surrender.

Why?

Because surrendering to God allows God to live here in earth through you. It allows God to fulfil His vision without you and your flesh getting in the way of that vision. It allows for as many as possible to be saved and to spend eternity with the Father.

And isn't that the goal?

God's goal?

Therefore, when we surrender everything we have and are to God, we are allowing God to exhibit His perfect love through us.

Love without restraint.

Love without compromise.

Love without limits.

Surrender is the perfect response to Christianity, God's call for us to love.

CHAPTER TWELVE

Christianity Requires Restoration.

Brethren, if a man be overtaken in a fault,
ye which are spiritual, restore such an one in the spirit of meekness;
considering thyself, lest thou also be tempted.
Galatians 6:1 (KJV)

Finally, because we have established that love is much more than warm, fuzzy feelings felt toward an individual, and that love is an action verb and thus requires action, it is now time to add that the love of which we have spoken and the surrender of which we have spoken is *all* for the act of restoration. It is for us to lead others to Christ so that Christ can restore them to God.

Just as He did with us.

Restoration is the act of returning something to a former owner, place, or condition. In Christianity, restoration is the act of returning people to God and to the state God originally created us to be in.

It's that simple.

Yet many don't understand it.

To make it understandable, we must first ask ourselves a question. What state did God create us to be in? For that answer, we should go back to the beginning, to the creation, to Adam, to Eve, and to The Garden of Eden.

In the beginning, when God created us, we were in a spiritual state. We knew God personally, we knew His voice, and we communicated with Him extensively. So much so that God talked to Adam, allowing Adam to name each and every animal. We knew God. We knew His Spirit. We had no knowledge of good and evil.

We were spiritually minded.

How do we know this?

Because scripture states that God is a spirit.

God is a Spirit:
and they that worship him must worship him in spirit and in truth.
(John 4:24 KJV)

Because God is a spirit, we had to talk to Him in the spirit. We had to interact with Him in the spirit. We had to see Him in the spirit. We had to know Him in the spirit. We had to **_be_** in the spirit. Just as we do now. And being in the spirit with God who is a spirit kept us at constant *oneness* with Him.

The way He wanted it to be.

Adam and Eve were so spiritually minded that they even heard God walking in the garden looking for them after Adam ate of the fruit. Who, today is so spiritually minded that you can hear God, the spirit that is God, coming toward you?

Not very many of us.

Why?

Because when Adam ate from the tree of the knowledge of good and evil, they became more fleshly and far less spiritual. Now, there was no such thing as oneness with God in the spirit. After all, how could they be one with God in the spirit when their attention was now divided between the spirit and the flesh? They were torn between two things whereas before the fruit they were only consumed with one. The spirit. Therefore, their connection to and with God had been compromised and a need to reconnect now existed.

You see, the soul is made up of the mind, the will, and the emotions. The soul is mostly about pleasing self, about pleasing the flesh. The spirit is all about pleasing God. Pre-fruit, they were all about the spirit, post-fruit they were mostly all about the flesh. They were no longer one with God. They were divided between being one with God and being one with their flesh. Therefore, Jesus is and had to be the source of the reconnect, the source that leads us back to God.

That is what restoration is and that is the reason why restoration is necessary.

Who Should We Restore?

We should restore God's people just as Christ restored us.

However, this is where things can become really difficult.

You see, walking like Christ calls for you to love your brothers and sisters to such a degree that if you see them overwhelmed by, or overtaken in, a fault, you sincerely wish to lead them in the righteous direction. It requires you to see someone doing something that can hurt them, hurt the Kingdom, or mar their relationship with God, and for you, with and in wisdom, to restore them, to correct them, to admonish them.

The love we have for them, for our fellow man, should be too great to see them hurt in any way, especially in a spiritual way. If we see a stumbling block, we should do all we can to remove it or to help them remove it. If we see a hindrance, we should try with everything in us to eliminate it. So, restoring those we love is a good thing, but only if it's coming from a place of love.

Godly love.

How We Should Restore.

There are many ways in which we can restore people to God. We can use our words, which many of us do. We can use our actions, which many of us fail to do. And we can use our prayers, which seems easiest of them

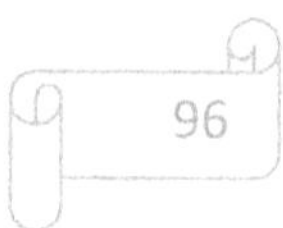

all. However, no matter what we choose to use as a method of restoring our brothers and sisters, we should always do it humbly, meekly, gently, with respect, and from a place of love.

Verbal Restoration.

When it comes to our words, not only should we humbly and with respect admonish our brothers and sisters in Christ, but we should also explain why we are admonishing them. It's hard enough telling someone that they are doing something that might be wrong, but going at them without scripture, without a thorough explanation of what they are doing wrong and how it negatively affects them and the church can and often does create results the complete opposite of what the desired goal is.

However, even when coming from a place of love, there are those who will perceive your verbal restoration as chastisement, as reprimanding, and who won't receive that well. There are some who will despise rebuke and admonishment. They will despise you telling them anything. They will be angry with you. They will scorn you. They will tell you to mind your own business. They will avoid you altogether. Because, after all, who do you think you are? Who are you to tell them anything? The last time they checked, you were only human just as they are. Nobody died and made you God. How dare you correct them when your life isn't perfect?

As challenging as this will be at times, we must recognize that they may not be aware that we are coming from a spiritual place, a place of love. We can't become angry or frustrated with them. We can't argue with them or debate with them. And most importantly, we cannot give up on them. We must, with meekness, understand their lack of understanding or understand the mind state they are in.

At the same time, we must remember that understanding and agreeing are two completely different things. Understand them, do not agree with them in their wrongdoing. Understand why they may be doing what they are doing, but do not agree with what they are doing if what they're doing hinders or even stunts the growth of the church.

Furthermore, if in the process of restoring, they, in their lack of understanding, tell you to mind your own business, do that. Respect their wish to be left alone. Do not try to convince them to see things a certain way. Do not harass them. Do not judge them. Do not gossip about them. Do not embarrass them. Do not try to force the word down their throats or choke them with it. Respect their space in the flesh, but in the spirit, when you are praying, use your words to *pray for them.*

Physical Restoration.

Action.

One of the ways in which you can restore a person is by the actions you do and don't take. You see, when you are living righteously in the presence of one who may not be living righteously, they will see this. Oftentimes, your righteous actions can convict a person, making them painfully aware that their own actions are and can be harmful not only to themselves, but also to others.

Think about it this way: There is a war going on between God and Satan. The war is being fought for the souls of man. God wants all of man to be saved. Satan wants all of man to be condemned. God uses His Spirit to save souls and restore them to Him. Satan uses the world and sin to keep souls disconnected from God. God loves you and wants to save you from Satan. The devil hates you and wants to keep you disconnected from God.

The weapons God and Satan use in this war are people.

God uses people for good.

Satan uses people for evil.

What people are they using?

You, and the people around you.

How are they using the people?

By their actions. By their good actions or by their bad actions.

Just because you believe in Christ does not mean you are automatically fighting on God's side and doing that which is good. On the contrary, just because a person does not believe in Christ, just because a person is unsaved, does not mean they are automatically fighting on Satan's side and doing what is bad.

It is your actions that determine whose side you are fighting on. It is your actions that determine if God is using you as a weapon of love, of peace, and of restoration. At the same time, is it also your actions that determine if Satan is using you as a weapon of mass destruction.

You see, those who do good, *what God calls good,* are fighting on the side of God. Those who do evil, those who do what the world calls good, or those who do *their own kind of good,* are fighting on the side of Satan. God's good is those things that are done to save souls, those things that will have you and others included in salvation, included in Heaven. Satan's good, or your own kind of good, is those things that are done to make people feel good and feel included in this world. However, we must remember that a friend of the world is the enemy of God.

> *Ye adulterers and adulteresses, know ye not that the friendship of the world is enmity with God? whosoever therefore will be a friend of the world is the enemy of God.*
> *(James 4:4 KJV)*

Thus, good is not determined by you or by people or by the world. Good is determined by your Godly actions and what your Godly actions lead to. Therefore, the good you do, the actions you take must be in compliance with God and His word and not with the world and for the world's approval.

We should also be painfully aware that in this war there is no such thing as middle ground. You are either fighting for God or you are fighting for Satan. No one is sitting this war out. If you believe you are not fighting on either side, you are still fighting for the devil.

Why?

Because by doing nothing you are *still not* fighting with God!

Thus, the question you should be asking yourself is whose side are you fighting on?

When you use your actions to lead people to Christ who will restore them to God, you are definitely allowing God to use you to fight on His side. When you use your actions to only make people feel good while they are here, to *only* please the flesh while they are here, you are definitely fighting on the side of Satan.

When your actions are righteous, they are being used in this war to reconnect souls to God. When your actions are unrighteous, they are being used to disconnect people or to help remain disconnected from God.

There is no middle ground.

So how do you use your actions to restore people to God?

You behave righteously while in their presence. You do what God tells you to do, allowing them to see that God's righteousness still exists in this world. You also use your actions to protect them, to keep them from knowing or experiencing worldly things that could lead them to condemnation.

You protect them from seeing wrong by letting them see you do right. You protect them from hearing the wrong things by speaking right things in their presence. You protect them from wrong thoughts by exposing their minds to right music, books, television shows, conversations, etc. You protect them from wrong emotions by tempering your emotions while in their presence.

You protect them.

Because you love them.

And because you're fighting for them on God's side.

And even if in the end they are still somehow exposed to unrighteousness, you and God will know that you did what God called you to do for them. And maybe, just maybe, that right that you did will one day lead them to Christ who will get them in right standing with God.

Restoration by Prayer.

As Christians, we should understand that whenever God allows us to see something unrighteous or wrong in or with others, it's not so that we can sit in judgement of them. It's not so that we can gossip about them. It's not so that we can condemn them. It's not so that we can think we are better than them. Allowing us to see the faults in others is done so that we can help them, so that we can restore them. However, if they do not want our help, if they reject our help, we should pray for them.

They can't reject our prayers because those are private conversations between us and God that they need not know anything about. And in those conversations we can ask God for everything for those we see in need of restoration that they will not allow us to tell them about or to help them with.

But why would we want to even pray for someone that has rejected our help?

Because we love them.

Because God loves them.

And because sometimes you can love someone more by praying for them than you ever can by talking to them.

Therefore, if need be, separate from them as they may wish and pray for them. Pray for the condition of their hearts. Pray for the condition of their souls. Pray for their relationship with God.

Why We Should Restore.

The reason we should restore is a very simple one. Everything about Christianity is based on restoration. As Christians, once we accept Christ into our lives we are restored to God. Once we are restored to God, we are supposed to utilize our Christianity to ensure that others accept Christ and thus are restored to God as well.

Christianity is all about restoration.

It is all about delivering us from sin and restoring us to the righteous state Adam was in before Adam committed sin. It is about living lives that reflect righteousness so that others can see that God is a restorer. It is about calling others to Christ so that He can restore them to God. Everything about Christianity is based on restoration, thus we should do all we can to restore as many as we can.

Why?

Because God restores us, and we should restore others.

Because God loves us and we in turn love Him and His people.

It's as simple as that.

As simple as Christianity.

As simple as responding to God's call to love!

XIII

CHAPTER THIRTEEN

What Christianity Is Not

And beside this, giving all diligence, add to your faith virtue; and to virtue knowledge;
And to knowledge temperance; and to temperance patience; and to patience godliness;
And to godliness brotherly kindness; and to brotherly kindness love.
For if these things be in you, and abound,
they make you that ye shall neither be barren nor unfruitful in the knowledge of our Lord
Jesus Christ. But he that lacketh these things is blind,
and cannot see afar off, and hath forgotten that he was purged from his old sins.
Wherefore the rather, brethren, give diligence to make your calling and election sure:
for if ye do these things, ye shall never fall:
For so an entrance shall be ministered unto you abundantly
into the everlasting kingdom of our Lord and Saviour Jesus Christ.
(2nd Peter 1:5-11 KJV)

We have spent a great deal of time learning what Christianity is and how to live like Christians, however, there are a few other things about Christianity that we should also explore.

Things like what Christianity is not.

The first thing Christianity is not may offend many, but offensive or not, it is the truth.

Christianity is not a religion.

At least not in the sense that some of you think religion is.

You see, in the Bible, religion is defined as **ceremonious** in worship.

<u>Ceremonious</u> – Formal and serious, suitable for a **ceremony**.

<u>Ceremony</u> – Observance of an established code of civility or politeness.
A formal act or event that is a part of a social or religious occasion.
Very polite or **formal** behavior.

<u>Formal</u> – Belonging to or constituting the form or essence of a thing.
Relating to or involving the outward form, structure, relationships, or arrangement of elements rather than content.

As we can clearly see from these definitions, in Christianity religion is a *form*-al and physical expression of the **essence** of God.

<u>Essence</u> – The basic, ultimate, and real nature of a thing.
The properties, quality, or qualities that make a thing what it is.

Religion is a demonstration of Godliness, a physical demonstration of what and who God really is. It is a form of worship that is both performed and observed through the behavior we, Christians, exhibit. Religion is Christians showing the true nature of God through the lives we live, lives that worship God. Others should see that performance of worship in all that we do. *That* is the religion that Christianity is, and our behavior should be performed sincerely, genuinely, and *religiously* whether we are within the walls of a church or not.

For the grace of God that bringeth salvation hath appeared to all men,
Teaching us that, denying ungodliness and worldly lusts, we should live soberly,
righteously, and godly, in this present world;
(Titus 2:11-12 KJV)

Christianity is a relationship with the Father, and the Son, and the Holy Spirit, a relationship that is walked out and lived out daily. It is *not* something we do for show or just to be seen. It is *not* something we simply attain yet do nothing with it. It is *not* something that is simply performed without meaning or even direction. Christianity is serious and for a very specific purpose. It is for the purpose of love, the purpose of bringing souls to Christ who will reconcile them to God.

And all things are of God, who hath reconciled us to himself by Jesus Christ, and hath given to us the ministry of reconciliation; To wit, that God was in Christ, reconciling the world unto himself, not imputing their trespasses unto them; and hath committed unto us the word of reconciliation. Now then we are ambassadors for Christ, as though God did beseech you by us: we pray you in Christ's stead, be ye reconciled to God.
(2ⁿᵈ Corinthians 5:18-20 KJV)

Christianity is *not* an excuse to bully people. Christ never bullied anyone, He spoke the truth to them and allowed them to decide whether or not they were going to believe His truth, *the truth*, and follow His truth on their own. You see, God wants people to come to Him because they want to, not because they have been bullied into Him or terrified into Him or even forced into Him. He wants you because He loves you. He wants you to love Him sincerely and He wants you to come to Him because you want to.

Think about it as if it were a relationship. Do you want someone to be with you because they were forced to be with you? Manipulated into being with you? Tricked into being with you? Threatened or frightened into being with you?

The majority of us would say no.

We want someone to be with us because of us, because they love us and genuinely want us in their lives. Well, the same applies to Christ, to God. He wants us to come to Him because our hearts and minds are with

Him, not out of obligation or out of fear. Because a relationship that is based on obligation or fear or manipulation is not a relationship at all. It is actually a farce, a fake joining together to fulfil a duty, to prevent or eliminate a fear, or to ease a pressured mind.

It is not real.

It is not of free will.

And it is not out of love.

> *But as it is written, Eye hath not seen, nor ear heard,*
> *neither have entered into the heart of man, the things which God hath prepared for*
> *them that love him.*
> *(1 Corinthians 2:9 KJV)*

Christianity is not a weapon we use to get people under our rule or under our control. It is not a weapon used to get people to think and behave as we wish them to. Never once did Christ wield His love like a weapon. He offered it and either you accepted it or you didn't. Even when they went against Him as Judas did, He did not once condemn Judas or speak a negative word against him or anyone who went against Him.

Christ simply obeyed God.

In fact, Christ didn't condemn the woman caught in adultery when the rest of the world wanted to condemn her. He demonstrated His love by asking her not to sin anymore and loved her by *not* condemning her. Had Christ condemned her and ostracized her, the people in the world of which she lived would have condemned her to death.

And how would that have given her a chance at salvation?

It would not have.

Thus, the love Jesus showed her not only saved her life, but it could have also saved her soul which is what we are all called to do.

Why?

Because we can lead many more souls to Christ by loving them than we ever can by hating them or by condemning them or by using our Christianity as a weapon against them.

> *So when they continued asking him, he lifted up himself, and said unto them, He*
> *that is without sin among you, let him first cast a stone at her.*
> *And again he stooped down, and wrote on the ground.*
> *And they which heard it, being convicted by their own conscience, went out one by one,*
> *beginning at the eldest, even unto the last: and Jesus was left alone, and the woman*
> *standing in the midst.*

Christianity is not an elite club.

Christianity is not a club of the best people that gives its members the right to hate people because they don't believe the same as the club members do. As Christians, we speak and live the word of God the way we should and those who accept it, we help to get as close to Christ as possible. Those who do not accept it, we allow them the same free will God gives them while still walking Christ-like in their presence.

They may not want to hear our words about Christ, but they can't stop our Christian lifestyle. They can't stop us from showing them Christ with every move we make. As long as we are walking in love and they are around us, they will not only see God in motion, but they will be presented with chance after chance to receive God's love. The same chances God presented us with the many times He presented us with them.

Christianity is not something you do while playing by your own set of rules. You don't change the Bible to fit your lifestyle and claim that you are a Christian. You don't redefine Christianity or scripture to better suit you and your needs and your wants. Because by redefining scripture to suit you, you are changing the reflection of God to the reflection of *you* and you are demonstrating Him to the world as what and who He is not.

Christianity means you are a follower of Christ. Following Christ means you live how He lived while obeying God the way He did, or you strive to with as much as is in you to do so.

You don't change the Bible.

And you don't reflect Christ falsely, thereby giving Him and Christianity a bad name.

God gave you the Bible. The Bible gives you the guidelines to live by. Those guidelines give you an accurate reflection of Christ to demonstrate to the world. That reflection of Christ draws others to Him. Those that are drawn to Him, He directs to God. And those directed to God are reconciled to God by the saving of their souls.

If you accept those guidelines, you gain the rewards that come with them. If you don't accept them, you gain the penalty that comes without them. It's that simple. There is no forcing anything, especially since God gives us all free will.

The way we spend our eternity is our choice.

God didn't take our choice from us and we shouldn't take the choice from others.

We either accept and live the truth of God and the truth of who God is or we don't, but we don't change the truth to fit us.

Because that, when they knew God, they glorified him not as God, neither were thankful; but became vain in their imaginations, and their foolish heart was darkened. Professing themselves to be wise, they became fools, And changed the glory of the uncorruptible God into an image made like to corruptible man, and to birds, and fourfooted beasts, and creeping things. Wherefore God also gave them up to uncleanness through the lusts of their own hearts, to dishonour their own bodies between themselves: Who changed the truth of God into a lie, and worshipped and served the creature more than the Creator, who is blessed for ever. Amen.
(Romans 1:21-25 KJV)

Christianity is *not* about *your own definition of right* or about doing *your own definition of good* the way you want to and for the reasons you want to, reasons *you think are right*. Christianity is about doing God's definition of right and God's definition of good because He calls you to.

Whatever we do for others, the love we give to others, is so that we can lead them to Christ, not so that we can *just* make them feel good. The love we give to others is for a reason that is much deeper than *just* the pleasure of their lifetime which is fleeting. The goodness and love we give to others is for the protection of their eternity.

Our love should not be to *just* please them temporarily, it should be to save them eternally. We should care about their forever, not *just* their right now.

There is a way that seemeth right unto a man, but the end thereof are the ways of death.
(Proverbs 16:25 KJV)

Christianity is not an excuse to ostracize those who do not believe or those who do not behave the way you want them to or think they should. In fact, those who do not believe are the people that need the love of God the most.

Why?

Because without Christ they are eternally separated from God. To remove yourself, the *Christ*-ian, from them is to take the love of Christ away from them, the love that should be living inside of you, the love that is meant not only for you, but for them as well. And how can Christ love someone *through you,* how can Christ call someone to Him through you if you have ostracized them?

He can't.

It is for that reason that you should not ostracize anyone. You love them unless they leave you alone or tell you to leave them alone.

Ostracizing them because of their behavior, because of what they celebrate, because of what they believe, because of what they say, because of how they live, is also *not* Christian behavior. Those who do not behave Christ-like need to be around those who *do* behave Christ-like so that they can see what Christ looks like, what He behaves like, how Christ loves them, and how those behaviors work for their good and for the good of Christianity and the church.

Does this Godly love mean that you should remain in the presence of a person that is hurting you or that means you harm?

No.

If a person is hurting you or harming you, *that* is a reason to remove yourself from their presence. Not so that you can ostracize them, however, but so that you, by removing yourself from them, can stop them from hurting you and thereby being a stumbling block and a hindrance to your Christianity and to their own.

Why?

Because even though they are hurting you, you still love them just as God does.

Christianity is *not* about harming and controlling others. Instead, it's about freeing others with the use of love. It's about the saving of souls. It's about loving God's people and it's about loving God. Christianity *is* a call to love, it is not the ostracizing of those that differ from us.

And it came to pass, as Jesus sat at meat in the house, behold, many publicans and sinners came and sat down with him and his disciples. And when the Pharisees saw it, they said unto his disciples, Why eateth your Master with publicans and sinners? But

And just as God called Christ to save us all through the use of love, Christ calls us to do the same for others.

Why?

Because Christianity is *not* a call to condemnation or confusion, it *is* a call to love.

Amen.

AFTERWORD

Christianity.

The thing that I take most seriously in my life.

The thing that I am most dedicated to.

However, never in a million years would I have ever thought that God would call me to write about it. Not that I am unable to write or anything like that, but because to me, Christianity is serious business, and this was a huge undertaking. An undertaking that I felt someone bigger in the Christian community should be called to do.

However, when God called me to do it, I did it.

Why?

Because He called me.

And that calling meant that He not only trusted me to do it, but that He equipped me to do it.

So, I tucked away my fears and doubts, trusted God, and let the writing begin.

I also did it because what He called me to do was my calling.

Writing.

Writing for God.

All of my life I'd had a heart for people, for justice for people. And what is more heart felt than writing something that introduces people to Christ? What is more just than setting them free from captivity by loving them unto salvation?

Nothing.

That's why I did it.

However, there's still more to it.

I was tired of Christianity being reflected in a negative and false light. I was tired of people dying spiritually and not even knowing it. I was tired of very few people knowing what Christianity really was and I was tired of Christianity being attacked because few people knew what it really was and reflected it properly. I was tired of Christianity being under fire and I was even more tired of why it was happening.

Thus, I set out on a mission to let people know that what they thought Christianity was and what it really is are two completely different things. I set out on a mission to enlighten the masses, to elicit salvation and to provoke as many as possible to love. I allowed God to pen this through me and in the process, I grew by leaps and bounds, just as I hope every reader of this book does.

It is my sincerest desire that every time this book is opened, God is seen and gets the glory. Every time this book is opened, I pray that the love of God comes shining through. And every time this book is opened, I pray that a soul is saved.

And to those who do not believe or who refuse to believe, to them I say, "Would you rather spend your life believing there is a God, die, find out there is no God, and simply spend eternity dead? Or would you rather spend your life believing there is *no* God, die, find out there *is indeed* a God, and spend eternity suffering tremendously?

The choice is yours.

But as for me and my house, we will serve the Lord.

And if it seem evil unto you to serve the Lord, choose you this day whom ye will serve; whether the gods which your fathers served that were on the other side of the flood, or the gods of the Amorites, in whose land ye dwell: but as for me and my house, we will serve the Lord.
(Joshua 24:15 KJV)

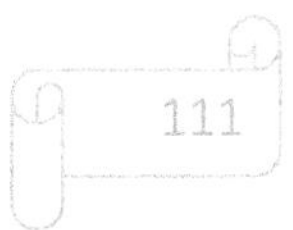

~A. B. Brumfield~